Strategic
Entrepreneurism™

Strategic

Entrepreneurism™

Shattering the Start-Up Entrepreneurial Myths

Jon B. Fisher

Gerald A. Fisher, Ph.D.

Wallace Wang

SelectBooks, Inc.
New York

Strategic Entrepreneurism™: Shattering the Start-Up Entrepreneurial Myths

This edition published by SelectBooks, Inc.
For information address SelectBooks, Inc., New York, New York.

First Edition

ISBN 978-1-59079-189-9

Library of Congress Cataloging-in-Publication Data

Fisher, Jon B., 1972-
Strategic entrepreneurism : shattering the start-up entrepreneurial myths
/ Jon B. Fisher, Gerald A. Fisher, Wallace Wang. -- 1st ed.
p. cm.
Summary: "Discusses the way to design a startup company specifically with
the goal of being acquired by a larger one"--Provided by the publisher.
ISBN 978-1-59079-189-9 (hardbound : alk. paper)
1. New business enterprises--Planning. 2. Entrepreneurship. 3.
Consolidation and merger of corporations--Planning. I. Fisher, Gerald A.
(Gerald Allen) II. Wang, Wally. III. Title.
HD62.5.F5328 2008
658.1'1--dc22
2008031658

Printed in the United States of America

10 9 8 7 6 5 4 3 2

This book is dedicated to Gerald, Anita, Danielle, Dave, Reido, Peter, Alice, Coleen, Ray, Barry, Dexter, Dennis, Jerry, John, Umang, Hank, Thomas, Bosco, Phil, Tony, and my favorite, Darla.

Contents

Introduction
The Real Life of an Entrepreneur

There's an old saying that if you don't know where you're going, you'll probably never get there. This is particularly true for starting a company. If you're going to start a company, you're probably going to think big. The ultimate dream of every entrepreneur is to create the next big success story. Whether you want to create a company that sells a specific product (such as Apple's iPhone) or provides a unique service (such as Google's search engine), the one key to starting up any company is that you must make money so your company can grow, thrive, and ultimately dominate its market.

Unfortunately, the odds of success may seem stacked against you from the start. For every 100 companies that start up every year, 98 of them will never raise enough money to get off the ground. Out of the remaining two ventures that do manage to get start-up money (often called "seed capital"), the odds are 90 percent that they will fail despite any amount of funding they may receive. Out of the few ventures that manage to stagger past this high failure rate, another 6 percent may go out of business within three years while 3 percent may become a moderate success. Less than 1 percent of all startups ever survive long enough to go public through an IPO (Initial Public Offering).

But even an IPO is no guarantee of future success. Wall Street is littered with the wrecks of once-hot IPOs that fizzled and disappeared or survived only long enough for another company to buy their assets for pennies on the dollar. If your ultimate dream is to turn your startup into the next Google or Apple, you might succeed, but the odds are so heavily stacked against you that it's more likely that you may never receive any compensation for all your hard work. In today's business climate, there are so many factors out of your control that chance plays a huge part of any successful IPO. This makes the idea of starting up the next Google or Apple possible, but statistically improbable.

Of course, just because something is improbable doesn't mean you shouldn't strive for that kind of success. The problem with trying to become the next household corporate name is that too often entrepreneurs view this as an all or nothing proposition. They believe that you have to shoot for the moon to succeed. If they don't succeed in achieving this lofty goal, their company, which they worked so hard to create, develop, and maintain, usually crashes and burns into bankruptcy.

Given a choice between becoming the next Google or Apple, or going out of business entirely and fading into obscurity, is it any wonder that so many startups fail miserably? If you try to hit home runs every time you step up to bat, you're going to strike out nearly as often as you hit a home run. In the world of sports, you can strike out and step up to the plate over and over again. In the world of business, one or two strikeouts can wipe you out financially so that you may never get another chance to correct your mistakes and succeed.

By following the old rules of starting up a company, you have to shoot for that one in a million shot if you want to succeed, even though the odds may be stacked heavily against you. If you can free yourself from the blinders of these old rules, you'll find that you always have other options for starting up a company. This new way of starting up a company, which I call Strategic Entrepreneurism (SE), can maximize your chance of success while minimizing your risks.

The basic idea behind Strategic Entrepreneurism is to refocus your goal. Instead of trying to become the one dominant company in your market, Strategic Entrepreneurism says that you want to be the one company that a larger and more dominant company wants to acquire.

From day one, create and design your company to become an attractive acquisition candidate. Identify the companies that you believe would most benefit from acquiring your company. Of course, you can never control what another company does, but by understanding which companies may acquire you and what their own needs may be, you can steer your company in their direction as an acquisition target. Then when your company gets acquired by a larger corporation, everyone will remark about how lucky you are, not knowing that this was your goal from the beginning.

After you understand how Strategic Entrepreneurism works, you'll never look at starting up a company the same way again.

THE REAL LIFE OF AN ENTREPRENEUR

Being an entrepreneur really means taking action. You don't necessarily need an MBA, or any college degree at all (although it can help). What you really need as an entrepreneur is a lot of guts, faith, trust, and support from people around you. What you do with all these ingredients is up to you.

When you're the boss, all responsibility falls on your shoulders. It's not always easy and not always fun. Even worse, it's not always financially rewarding either, especially if your company goes belly up and dies before your eyes. However, being the boss means you get to call the shots; you get to define the direction for your company, and you get to reap the rewards of your efforts. If you're looking for job security with plenty of paid vacation time and a fixed time limit for working, you won't find it as an entrepreneur. If you're looking for a way to express your creativity and play the game of business on a large scale while making a difference in the world, then being an entrepreneur may be for you.

The dream of an entrepreneur is to have success and to enjoy the fruits of that success. When I ran Bharosa, our law office had a sweeping view of the entire San Francisco Bay. On particularly stressful days, my cofounders and I would stare out the windows to watch the fantastic yachts glide serenely across the water on a weekday afternoon. That's when we'd wistfully look at each other and then out at the yachts and tell ourselves, "That guy closed."

That meant that whoever was piloting that yacht had probably sold his company for millions of dollars and now had all the time he wanted to relax and enjoy life on his million-dollar yacht on a Wednesday afternoon. While it was more likely he inherited the money, it was nice for us to imagine he was one of us.

So many entrepreneurs have achieved massive success and there's no reason why you can't do it too. However, let me caution you that being an entrepreneur isn't all about making an unbelievable amount of money without doing much hard work. If you want to be an entrepreneur, you must love being an entrepreneur or be driven and ambitious enough to choose this path, because it won't always be easy.

My wife clearly remembers the day she returned home to find me dripping with my own perspiration because of the pressure and activity of the day. I had a large rash under each arm and down my sides from the perspiration. She wanted to take me to the hospital, but a cold shower and dinner at a nice restaurant helped me unwind and relax long enough for the rash to fade away on its own.

I still have framed MRI scans of my body on my office desk taken at the conclusion of each of my ventures. I have an L5S1 (left disk protrusion) in my lower back that causes significant pain in my left leg, which was caused from too much running on treadmills and possibly from long hours sitting at my desk at Bharosa.

I also have a scan of my neck and head resulting from a severe neck strain from the stress of running my second company, NetClerk.

One time I had been asked to give a report on Internet operations (as head of Internet operations) to the board of directors of a 3000 employee company (AutoReach/Tasha). I was 23 years old at the time and was cut off after speaking just 90 seconds. (The company even fired me six weeks later.)

In addition to the physical stress one must endure, succeeding as an entrepreneur requires being able to perform under pressure. I have walked into meetings knowing I needed to convince the attendees to invest $10 million in my company or I would have to fire 30 percent of my employees. I have sat across the table with the largest enterprise and most acquisitive software company in the world, and answered a barrage of questions knowing that each answer was putting my own money at stake.

I don't want to discourage anyone from becoming an entrepreneur, but I don't want you to think that being an entrepreneur is a path to easy money. It takes a lot of work, a lot of persistence, a lot of determination, and a lot of courage. I did it and I survived, so that means you can do it too. Just keep your eyes wide open and understand that the life of an entrepreneur may not be easy, but it can certainly be worth it.

MY LIFE STORY
(as told by the *San Jose Business Journal*)

To get to know who I am, it's probably best to read about my past from an objective point of view, in this case, from the *San Jose Business Journal*, which has printed various stories about my different companies:

Friday, June 28, 1996

ONLINE AUTOS: Fremont's Tasha Automotive Group has joined AutoReach Inc., a leading car leasing and buying service on the Internet, to put its fleet of Chryslers, Hondas, Lexuses, Nissans and Toyotas on the information superhighway.

Tasha has 12 dealerships and 17 franchises in the Bay Area. It was the region's largest car dealer last year, with $529 million in sales. The company hopes to boost its record of 25,000 new and used vehicles sold by adding cyberspace to its territory.

*****

Friday, September 17, 1999
Internet venture NetClerk Inc. has signed on a group of blue-chip investors to wage a war on red tape.

The South San Francisco startup is taking aim at an obscure niche, helping home contractors comply with local government building regulations, but nevertheless has attracted participation from Oracle President Ray Lane, BroadVision CEO Pehong Chen, Verisign CEO Stratton Sclavos and Keynote Software CEO Umang Gupta. That group and a handful of founders and other investors have scraped together $1.3 million to build a site and services that will begin testing in six Bay Area counties next week.

The system will allow small contractors, including plumbers, electricians and roofers, to process routine permit applications electronically on the NetClerk web site, which customizes the submissions to meet the requirements of local jurisdictions. In its initial rollout, NetClerk employees will suffer the various quirks of local records offices, but ultimately the company aims to help those offices standardize to a more efficient electronic model.

NetClerk is an example of second-generation web companies that are not necessarily targeting multibillion-dollar markets, but seek to own lucrative niches by meeting specific needs. So rather than aiming for a big venture capital war chest right away, the company took a strategic approach in lining up key allies at the same time it proved its product.

"The core offering needs to succeed immediately to prove its worth, but we think we can quickly establish a destination site for contractors," said Jon Fisher, founder and CEO of NetClerk, adding that expansion into other markets will occur early next year. The company's niche focus was attractive to its entrepreneurial investors in a way that may not have immediately struck the fancy of venture capitalists on the prowl for the next mass-market score. While an initial minimum venture financing in the e-commerce realm now hovers in the $5 million area, Fisher recognized the importance of establishing credibility before capital.

"I think the future successful startups in the Internet space are mostly going to be companies that provide a unique service with a sustainable business model," said Gupta, an early Oracle executive and founder of two public companies. "I felt I could help them because of my entrepreneurial experience and their eagerness to learn."

Fisher approached Gupta because he is a director of his and partner Phil Wohl's high school alma mater. He found the other investors through similarly personal ties.

Fisher said the $1.3 million has allowed an early build out of the system to prepare its launch, but that it now believes it is ready to take its message to the venture capitalists.

"We anticipate we will raise at least $5 million by the end of the year to really begin to scale the product," Fisher said.

*****

Friday, October 8, 2004
A start-up in Santa Clara today is launching a new way for consumers to thwart online identity thieves without requiring them to install new hardware or software on their computers.

The company, Bharosa Inc., has designed a means of transmitting screen names and passwords without typing them on a keyboard, where phishers or hackers using key-logging programs could surreptitiously capture the data.

If Bharosa succeeds, it could put a big dent in phishing, the category of computer attack in which criminals set up fake bank or e-commerce sites to steal a computer user's personal information. Information security firm Symantec estimates that 1.78 million Americans have been caught by phishing expeditions over the last year that have cost banks and credit card issuers $1.2 billion.

Some security companies have been pushing a technology known as tokens—small keychain-style gadgets that display a new password every minute. In addition, Bharosa CEO Jon Fisher and Thomas Varghese, president and chief technology officer, expect that improvements in biometric systems that let users authenticate themselves with a fingerprint or a retinal pattern may become secure methods of identification. Still, they tout their technology as a hardware-free approach that is available right now.

"We can have this up and running at any Fortune 500 company in 30 days," Mr. Fisher says.

The two technology veterans came up with the concept at a Starbucks in San Mateo and jotted it down on a napkin.

That first design was a graphic representation of a combination lock. The user could make the dial on the lock spin by clicking on arrows to direct the wheel to turn clockwise or counter-clockwise. Clicking on "enter" would select the appropriate letter or number.

The beauty of this design, they say, is no keyboard activity for key-loggers to record. The only information sent over the Internet would be something like 20 degrees clockwise or 30 degrees counter-clockwise.

But there was a flaw to this design, Messrs. Fisher and Varghese realized: An attacker who captures the entire screen could see which letters and numbers are selected.

Eventually, a better idea occurred to Mr. Varghese—use two wheels instead of one.

Here's another way to picture it: Imagine two wheels, one inside the other. One has letters printed on it, the other numbers. Colored patches make pairs of the letters and numbers. Every time you go to a log-in screen, the wheels will have turned to form a new combination.

To sign on, a user locates the first letter or number of his password. If that initial letter lines up with the number "7" and the color yellow, then 7-yellow becomes the marker by which the rest of the password can be entered. The user then clicks on arrows to move that marker around to each additional character of the password, clicking on an "Enter" button to submit each letter or digit. Someone capturing the screen or looking over the user's shoulder would see two wheels rotating but would have no clue as to what their movement meant.

"It's just two wheels that interact in a way that only the user understands," says Mr. Varghese.

Bharosa plans to license its security wheel to banks, Internet service providers and e-commerce sites for $100,000 to $1 million, depending on the number of users. At least initially, Mr. Fisher believes, customers of client companies will be able to choose whether they wish to use the wheel for greater security. Bharosa is testing its concept with two large e-commerce companies and several large financial companies, says Mr. Fisher, although he will not reveal the names.

The privately held company has been self-funded and has some angel backing, Mr. Fisher says.

Analysts are interested, but cautious.

"This is a step in the right direction," says Gartner analyst Aviah Litan. But she still puts her security hopes in tokens. "In the end it's not a good substitute for a good card token," she says.

Users may also find it difficult to adjust to the new concept of circles instead of spaces to type passwords.

"It's hard to do real innovation on user interfaces," says Alex Aiken, professor of computer science at Stanford University. "People tend to acclimate slowly to new ideas and even small changes." And, he adds, "even now 10 percent of Internet surfers don't know how to use a scroll bar."

Still, the security industry acknowledges that something must change—and soon.

"There has been a dramatic increase of threats from piracy in general and spyware and key-logging in particular," says Oliver Friedrichs, senior manager of Redwood City-based Symantec Security Response. Symantec offers software designed to catch key-logging and spyware software that some attackers use to grab your information.

Other companies such as RSA and ActivCard have designed gadgets called keys, or tokens, that look like a digital pocket watch. Instead of telling time they display a number, which the user employs to log onto a Web site. The key is coordinated with the Web site's server, and the number it displays changes every minute. America Online recently adopted this method for its PassCode token program for subscribers who want to pay for added security.

Mr. Friedrichs sees these keyfob tokens as the most secure password technique.

"If it's just software running on a computer, it's not as secure as a token you have in your pocket," he says.

But Mr. Fisher wonders if the token idea will ever catch on.

"So people really want to carry around a token for online access to their bank and another for access to their Internet service and others for eBay and PayPal and Amazon?" he asks. "Our design is radically different and asks for new behaviors. But consumers don't have to keep track of various pieces of plastic. Adoption of our technology is simply a matter of saying 'yes.'"

WHO IS JON FISHER?

2007 was a great year.

That was the year I served as Bharosa, Inc.'s CEO until its successful acquisition by Oracle Corporation. For the next six months I worked as Vice President Product Management to integrate Bharosa within Oracle. My assignment with Oracle ended just in time for me to enjoy the holidays. Later I won Ernst & Young's Entrepreneur of the Year award in Silicon Valley and lectured across the country.

After 15 years as an entrepreneur, I also learned my most valuable business lesson about Strategic Entrepreneurism. To show you how important Strategic Entrepreneurism has been to my work, I would have gladly traded everything that materialized in 2007 if only I could have understood Strategic Entrepreneurism 10 years earlier.

Although Bharosa was my biggest success, I don't want you to get the idea that I got lucky or that I haven't had my share of failures, because neither is true. While luck always plays a part in any type of success, you can create your own luck by being prepared for opportunities as they arise. The main part of my success with Bharosa came about after I had already started up and worked as the CEO for two previous companies as well[1].

I started my first company while studying political science and economics at Vassar College and dropped out of school to run this company, which I later sold at age 23. Afterwards, I returned to school where I finished my degree in organizational behavior at the University of San Francisco.

After graduating I jumped into my second startup, which turned into a classic example of a company that had all the elements of success, but failed because of the simple mistake of

---

[1]My first two companies were AutoReach and NetClerk. AutoReach was later acquired by the Tasha Automotive Group, which merged with AutoNation. NetClerk failed and its assets were bought up by BidClerk.

sacrificing long-term strategic performance in exchange for short-term profits and growth. Of all the possible mistakes an entrepreneur can make, this can be the most fatal error that can doom a company since it comes disguised as a Trojan Horse masquerading as growth and increased revenue.

While every company should strive for growth and revenue, unchecked, rampant growth can actually choke a company and kill it by diverting limited resources towards multiple and tiny sources of income. You may think that as long as you're making money, you can never go broke, but if the cost of servicing and managing multiple, tiny income sources takes too much time and effort, you may never make much of a profit either.

The trick is to manage growth and revenue intelligently. You want maximum growth and profit that you can sustain now and in the long-term. It's one thing to get plenty of customers, but it's an entirely different thing to service those customers. McDonald's started selling hamburgers from a single restaurant and gradually branched out across the world, but imagine if in the beginning they had started trying to sell millions of hamburgers from their first restaurant. They would have been swamped with too many orders and not enough resources, so they would have wound up failing no matter how large their potential profits might have been.

By knowing how to recognize and avoid this problem of rapid growth, you can make the most crucial decision of an entrepreneur that can spell the difference between success or failure for any company. The lessons that I learned from my first two companies ultimately helped me create Bharosa correctly from the start.

Finally, luck had little to do with the fact that the sale of Bharosa to Oracle gave investors a six-fold return on their investment within a three-year time frame. (The typical successful startup delivers a three-fold return on an investment in five years, so Bharosa became twice as profitable in nearly half the amount of time.)

Bharosa, which had 25 million users at the time of its acquisition, was Oracle's 32nd purchase since its $10.3 billion takeover of PeopleSoft Inc. in January 2005. Oracle Chief Executive Officer Larry Ellison has spent more than $25 billion on his deals, making the company the most acquisitive in the software industry. On September 20, 2007, Larry Ellison even stated Oracle's long-term plan:

> Our strategy for growth is to find a way to add more value to the same customers we already serve, which are the large end of the mid-market and large companies. What we're doing here is moving beyond ERP to industry specific software. So in the telecommunications industry that would be billing systems and network provisioning systems and network inventory systems; core applications to run their business. Core applications to run a bank. Core applications to run a retail chain of stores. Core applications to run a utility. That's our focus, and that allows us to leverage the existing relationships that we have because we already sell databases to these companies, we sell middleware to these companies. We sell ERP and CRM to these companies, and now we want to sell this industry-specific software.

What allowed Bharosa to earn millions of dollars for me and my founding team was applying the principles of Strategic Entrepreneurism to all aspects of the company, from its inception all the way through its growth as a viable company. I knew what types of companies Oracle wanted to buy, so I made sure I made Bharosa into the exact type of company that Oracle would acquire. The principles of Strategic Entrepreneurism turned Bharosa into a success. I'm confident that these principles will work for any business, and now I'm going to share these principles with you.

1

The Basics of Entrepreneurism

Strategic Entrepreneurism is about designing your company, right from the start, toward a clear, definite outcome. When we created Bharosa, we designed the entire company to be acquired for the maximum amount of money in the shortest amount of time. Oracle didn't suddenly discover Bharosa and decide that my company would be a natural fit. Instead, we designed Bharosa to fit right into a company like Oracle from the beginning. Everything Bharosa did from day one was aimed at making the company an attractive acquisition target.

Practicing Strategic Entrepreneurism can actually involve more discipline than trying to build a company towards an IPO. First, you must rely on far less investment capital to guard against dilution. The more money you accept to start up your company, the more you'll have to pay back to these initial investors before you can make any money yourself.

Second, you must build your company's products so that they can be seamlessly integrated with a potential acquirer in mind. This can be as simple as making sure your product doesn't compete directly with a potential acquirer's product, to ensuring that customer contracts don't contain too much liability for an acquirer, to courting the right analysts to say and print just the right things about your company. If I could make only a single bet on my entire company, I would bet on the right customer (and the right team to serve that customer) who is of maximum strategic interest to a potential acquirer.

By making the correct decisions right from the start, all entrepreneurs can increase their chances of success for their company. However, to fully understand the advantages of Strategic Entrepreneurism, you must first understand what being an entrepreneur is all about.

BEING AN ENTREPRENEUR

The best part about becoming an entrepreneur is that you can make your own rules. Given a choice, most entrepreneurs would rather start their own company than work for somebody else. It's not that entrepreneurs can't work in a typical job, but that entrepreneurs enjoy making decisions to control their own destiny. A true entrepreneur isn't someone motivated solely by money or power, but by the desire to make a difference.

Although it's true that most entrepreneurs must work long hours, especially when trying to get their company off the ground, entrepreneurs aren't necessarily workaholics; they simply enjoy what they do. Some entrepreneurs enjoy working in specific industries, such as software or alternative energy. Other entrepreneurs simply enjoy the process of creating companies, no matter what field they may be in. To an entrepreneur money is just a way to measure how well they're playing the game of business.

Anyone can become an entrepreneur. Colonel Sanders became an entrepreneur at the age of 65 when he started Kentucky Fried Chicken. Michael Dell formed PC Limited (the predecessor to Dell Computers) from his dormitory at the University of Texas in Austin when he was only 19. Julie Aigner-Clark started the Baby Einstein Company from her suburban home in Denver, Colorado. Because entrepreneurs can make their own rules, they're not limited by age, race, sex, location, or educational background. If you have a good idea, believe in your dream, and have a lot of persistence, there's nothing that can stop you from becoming an entrepreneur too.

STRATEGIC ENTREPRENEURISM REQUIRES ENTREPRENEURS TO WORK IN TEAMS

While the media loves to highlight the accomplishments of individual entrepreneurs, the truth is that entrepreneurs rarely succeed on their own. Entrepreneurs usually succeed as part of a team of entrepreneurs.

At Bharosa we needed entrepreneurs with extraordinary dedication and work ethics way beyond the call of duty, so that Bharosa would need to raise less outside capital in order to suffer less dilution. Still, we needed to be able to compete with companies with significantly more resources, including significantly larger teams. The men who were perhaps our two finest entrepreneurs, Thomas Varghese, our founder and president, and our co-founder and VP engineering, Bosco Durai, led our product and engineering organizations that were responsible for critical execution. Bharosa's attractiveness to an acquirer like Oracle was in large part due to the quality and scalability of our products. Perhaps nothing was more important to Oracle than entrepreneurs like Thomas and Bosco.

Although the media portrays entrepreneurs as loners who tinker in a garage somewhere and hit it big overnight, the truth is that most entrepreneurs team up with at least one other person right from the start. The entrepreneur may have the technical skills needed to create a product or service, while the partner may possess the business skills needed to get the company off the ground (or vice versa).

For example, Bill Gates started Microsoft with his friend Paul Allen. While both men were programmers, Paul Allen is credited with making the business deal to purchase an operating system called QDOS for $50,000. This later became the MS-DOS operating system that Microsoft sold to IBM and other computer manufacturers.

Scott Cook founded the financial software company Intuit after realizing that personal computers could replace traditional paper and pencil accounting methods. Since at that time Scott Cook was a product manager for Proctor & Gamble, he enlisted the help of Tom Proulx, a programmer who could create the actual software known as Quicken. With Scott Cook handling the business affairs and Tom Proulx handling the programming chores, the two of them eventually turned Intuit into a billion dollar company.

The foundation of any company's success starts with the entrepreneur's vision, but achieving that goal requires a team who possesses the necessary skills to turn raw ideas into a concrete reality. Just as a quarterback can't win a football game by himself, so an entrepreneur can't succeed alone.

Every entrepreneur needs the right people on his or her team and every entrepreneur also needs the right mentors, who act like coaches. These mentors can give you advice and suggest different ways of thinking or studying problems. Mentors can be friends, acquaintances, or business associates, but whoever they might be, mentors are a necessary part of every entrepreneur's success.

Mentors can often provide an objective view of your current situation and give you advice from their own experience. Often mentors have gone through similar situations before, so they can help you identify opportunities and avoid pitfalls that you might have not seen otherwise. Although it's possible to startup and run a company without mentors, it's extremely difficult to go it alone. Mentors simply act like guides, showing you the shortcuts through a seemingly impenetrable jungle of confusion and opportunities.

Ultimately if you have the right idea but the wrong people, your plan for success will never get executed properly. If you have the right people but the wrong idea, you'll just move quickly in the wrong direction. The key to winning the game of business is to combine the right idea with the right people.

ENTREPRENEURS SOLVE PROBLEMS

Entrepreneurs don't just create companies for the sake of building a business. Entrepreneurs create companies to solve crucial problems for individuals or other businesses. By their very nature, entrepreneurs often find new ways to solve existing problems. As a result, entrepreneurs often avoid competing directly with existing companies and tackle problems that existing companies ignore or haven't recognized in the first place.

At one time, the only way to watch movies was to visit a theater or wait for the movie to appear on TV. After inexpensive videocassettes appeared, 29-year-old David P. Cook wanted to help people solve the problem of watching their favorite movies at home without having to buy them each time. So in 1985 he formed Blockbuster Video to make it inexpensive for people to rent the latest movies and watch them at their convenience at home.

Although the video rental business solved the problem of watching a movie at your convenience, it soon created another problem. Video rental stores like Blockbuster could offer only a limited selection of movies due to space restrictions in their stores. In 1997 Marc Randolph and Reed Hastings provided the solution to this problem by forming Netflix, a mail-order video rental service. Now consumers have the convenience of watching movies at home with the added convenience of having a virtually unlimited library of movies to choose from.

At the time of this writing, entrepreneurs are creating companies to solve the problem of having to wait for movies to arrive in the mail. Perhaps by the time you read this, some clever entrepreneur will find a way to make it easy to download movies directly to your television set, personal computer, or even a mobile device like a personal digital assistant or mobile phone. Then you can watch movies instantly, whether you're home or stuck in line waiting to get into a concert or ballgame.

Each new development, such as videocassettes and DVDs, spawns new opportunities and possible new solutions. Because the world is always changing, new opportunities are popping up all the time and new problems are created (and solved) every day. As a result, there will never be a shortage of opportunities for entrepreneurs to succeed.

LEVERAGING HIGH-TECHNOLOGY

There will always be new problems that require new solutions, which means the landscape for entrepreneurs will always be wide open. In general, there are two types of businesses you can start: a traditional brick-and-mortar business and a high-technology venture.

A traditional brick-and-mortar business requires physical resources such as a building and equipment. The building and equipment may not require a massive investment, but it does require a physical presence. Back in 1965 Fred De Luca borrowed $1,000 from family friend, Peter Buck, to start a sandwich shop when he was only 17 years old. Initially Fred wanted to earn enough money to pay for college, but when his sandwich shop proved popular, he expanded and franchised his restaurant. This eventually became the popular Subway restaurants, the third largest restaurant franchise behind McDonald's and Yum! Brands (which owns Kentucky Fried Chicken, Taco Bell, and Pizza Hut).

The biggest problem with a traditional brick-and-mortar business is the cost for starting up and the long period of time before such a business can grow from a good idea to a multimillion dollar company. Fred De Luca may have started Subway with $1,000, but he needed several decades to grow.

While there's nothing wrong with starting a brick-and-mortar business, another alternative is to start a high-tech business. The two biggest advantages of a high-tech business are the low startup costs and the potential for a high return on your investment in a short amount of time.

Wikipedia defines High-Technology as "technology that is at the cutting edge—the most advanced technology currently available." Basically, high-technology leverages your strengths and multiplies your potential profitability. For minimal cost and maximum potential success, take advantage of high-technology when starting up your company.

Back in 1996 Larry Page started a research project designed to study the number of links connecting various web pages. After showing friends his project, Larry with his collaborator Sergey Brin, soon formed the basis for a search engine that made searching the Internet faster and more accurate. Initially, this entire research project existed entirely on a single computer.

In 1998 Larry and Sergey incorporated his company as Google, and by 2000, Google had started earning revenue through online advertising. By 2004 Google had gone public and raised a market capitalization of more than $23 billion. In less than eight years Google went from an interesting project started on a university computer to a billion dollar company. In comparison, Subway took nearly forty years to reach a net worth of $1.5 billion dollars. There's no arguing with success, but given a choice, would you rather wait forty years to make $1.5 billion or wait eight years to make $23 billion?

Building a business around high-technology simply lowers your startup costs and increases your chance for massive profitability in the shortest amount of time. Instead of creating a physical product that needs to be made, shipped, and delivered, a high-technology business literally creates a product out of thin air.

In the case of Bharosa, we created a software authentication program that resides on a server (nothing for users to download). We needed to create Bharosa's program only once, and then we could duplicate it as many times as necessary at no added cost. Distributing our product could be done inexpensively electronically through the Internet.

The bulk of Bharosa's expenses went toward the physical cost of office space and employee salaries, which every company needs. But instead of spending additional money on a warehouse to store products, a factory to manufacture a product, or a trucking service to deliver the product to customers, Bharosa leveraged technology to eliminate those costs while increasing the speed of distribution at the same time. You can think of a high-tech company as a leaner, more efficient form of a traditional brick-and-mortar business but without the added expenses.

One reason why Netflix is killing Blockbuster's business is that Blockbuster is saddled with the cost of expensive retail stores while Netflix relies on the minimal cost of postage to deliver the products right to the customer's front door. By combining the low-tech use of the postal system with the high-tech use of databases to track and manage its massive inventory of movies stored on DVDs, Netflix can service far more customers at far less cost than Blockbuster can ever hope to do.

In many cases, a high-tech startup can compete with and dominate a traditional brick-and-mortar competitor (Netflix vs. Blockbuster) no matter how big the brick-and-mortar company may be, or how long it has been in business. Trying to compete with a brick-and-mortar business by opening another brick-and-mortar business is almost always a recipe for disaster. Hollywood Video tried to compete head-to-head with Blockbuster and lost. Burger King will probably never wipe out McDonald's, and Peet's Coffee will likely never wipe out Starbucks. Both Burger King and Peet's Coffee may be profitable, but if you're going to start any company, why settle for creating a company that practically guarantees you'll be forever stuck with second-rate status?

By leveraging high-technology in your business, either as your product itself or part of your service, you can create a nimble company that can service an untapped market, or provide a new service to an existing market. In either case, relying on high-technology lowers your cost of entry and helps you outmaneuver your competition to the point where you essentially have no competition. If you can carve out a niche for your company and establish your company as the leader in that niche, customers will have no choice but to turn to you.

HIGH-TECHNOLOGY + CREATIVITY = CAPITAL

Perhaps the most important use of high-technology is to leverage your own creativity. In the old days, companies measured capital by the things they owned. General Motors is worth billions of dollars because it owns so much real estate, buildings, equipment, and inventory. If General Motors shut down the company tomorrow, its assets would be worth a fortune, but once sold, it would be gone forever.

With a high-tech company, the assets aren't in physical items, but in intangible processes that are difficult for competitors to duplicate. Anyone can slap together the same parts to build a computer, which is why computer manufacturers like Gateway could not compete against Dell Computers and Hewlett-Packard. However, Apple doesn't just build computers; it also offers a unique sense of design and a synergistic ecosystem of products that not only work together, but convey a sense of being on the cutting edge of technology.

When you buy an Apple Macintosh computer, you're not only buying a physical product (the computer), but also Apple's brand

(Think Different) combined with Apple's unique software offerings that include iTunes (for easy integration with Apple's iPods) and synchronization features (for easy integration with Apple's iPhone).

The moment you buy one Apple product, it's easier to buy and use another Apple product since they work so well together. Companies such as Microsoft, Dell Computers, and Sony may try to compete with their own music players or colorful and stylish computer designs, but they'll always fall short of anything offered by Apple. By combining high-tech with their creativity, Apple has essentially raised the standards so high that it has effectively eliminated all of its competitors. If you want a computer, digital music player, or mobile telephone like the Macintosh, iPod, or iPhone, you have no choice but to buy one from Apple.

In today's world, the true value of a company doesn't lie in its physical assets but in its intellectual assets. Anyone can duplicate the physical parts of a company, but nobody can successfully copy the creativity of another company. Without high-tech, Ford can often successfully copy and duplicate anything created by General Motors and vice versa. By leveraging your unique creativity with high-tech, you enhance and multiply your creativity in ways that competitors can't easily follow. With high-tech, your true assets are nothing more than the unique way that you choose to do business with others.

ELIMINATE THE NEED TO CREATE
THE IMPOSSIBLE

One of the biggest fallacies of starting an entrepreneurial venture is that you need to create a new product or service that's radically different from anything currently on the market. The truth is that you don't need to invent something impossible like a car that runs on water or a new material that's stronger than steel but lighter than a piece of paper. To succeed in business, you just need to identify a problem with an existing business and find a way to make it better.

Given the high cost of gasoline, General Motors and Toyota took two different approaches. Back in 1997 General Motors developed and marketed an electric car dubbed the EV1. At the same time, Toyota introduced the Prius, a combination gasoline-electric hybrid car.

By 2003 General Motors had cancelled the EV1 despite growing demand and interest. In comparison, Toyota continued to improve on its hybrid engine technology to the point where the Prius has become the most popular alternate energy vehicle in the world.

Both Toyota and General Motors spent millions of dollars developing their technology, but General Motor's EV1 struggled with short endurance because of the limited amount of charge its batteries could hold, as Toyota's Prius simply advanced technology just a little bit to achieve the market success and profitability that eluded General Motors.

The lesson is simple. If you try to create a radically new product, your chances of failure are much greater than if you try to improve an existing product. Not only does improving an existing product take less time and money, but it also increases your ultimate chance for acceptance and success as well.

THE TYPICAL PATH OF A STARTUP

While every startup is different, the path for each startup consists of several distinct phases as shown in Figure 1-1. First, the entrepreneur dreams up an idea for a business. Second, the entrepreneur assembles a team to help create and market the product. With a team in place, the entrepreneur may need to raise seed

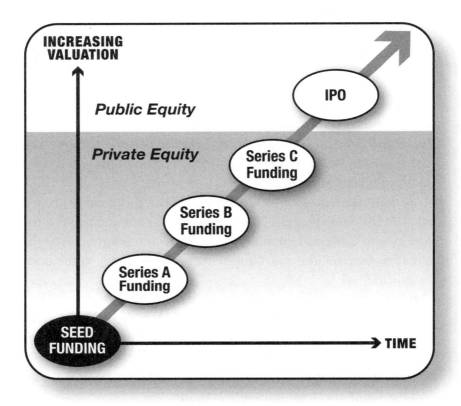

Figure 1-1. The Life Cycle of a Typical Startup

money to get the company started. This money can be the team's own money, money from friends and relatives, or money from outside investors.

As the company grows, it may go through additional rounds of funding, which provides money necessary for the company to continue growing. Ideally the profits generated by the company can provide the additional money necessary to continue growing, but if profits are trickling in, you may need this additional funding to move the company forward much faster. For example, you may need additional funding to pay for expanding your sales force or purchasing additional equipment.

Many companies make the mistake of using additional funding to pay their bills and keep the company alive. What inevitably happens is that the company continues losing money and once outside funding dries up, the company is forced to declare bankruptcy. As a general rule, startups should only use each round of additional funding to help it move forward, not to delay bankruptcy. During this period, a startup remains a private corporation.

After several rounds of funding, a startup may decide to offer an IPO that essentially allows anyone to buy shares in the company and become part owners. This is the time where a company becomes public. A successful IPO is generally considered a major milestone, although it's really just another form of additional funding.

In the traditional model, a startup's success relies on offering an IPO. However, the long path towards reaching an IPO can take years. During the dot-com bust of the '90s, many companies issued IPOs prematurely, watched their stock price skyrocket, and then plummet into nothing.

In Strategic Entrepreneurism, the goal isn't to reach an IPO but to sell out to an acquiring company much earlier. The drawback is that the potential valuation is much less, but the major advantage is that it takes less time, which also increases the chance of success, as shown in Figure 1-2.

The typical business model for a startup assumes that the longer a company stays in business, the higher its valuation, but that's not always true for two reasons. First, the longer a company stays in business, the greater the chance of failure, either through changing market conditions or growing competition. Second, the more funding your startup receives, the greater the dilution of ownership for the entrepreneur. The longer you hold on to a company, the greater the risk that your valuation may decrease.

Even worse, the longer you hold on to a company, the greater the risk that your company will never be profitable altogether.

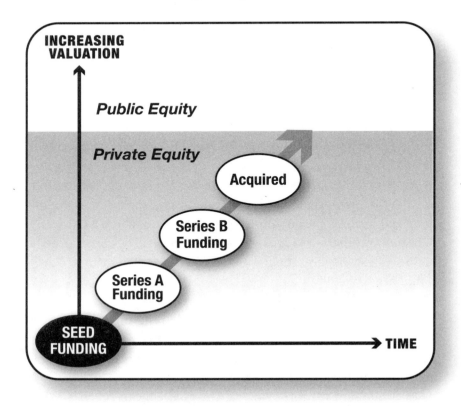

*Figure 1-2. Strategic Entrepreneurism Focuses a
Startup into Being Acquired Early in its Life*

On July 1, 2008, the National Venture Capital Association reported that in the second quarter of 2008, not a single venture-backed company staged an initial public offering, the first time this had occurred in 30 years.

The length of time that a venture-backed company goes from founding to IPO is now 8.6 years, which hit a 27-year high in 2007.

In considering the value of a company, you must examine the investors' returns as a function of time and value, not just value. $1.00 invested for 8.6 years must become $2.30 just to get an approximate 10% compounded return to give a nominal profit for investors. $1.00 must become $4.80 after 8.6 years for a compounded 20% return that makes a company profitable to most venture capitalists.

So the math is pushing venture capitalists to swing for the fences in every way, and yet the fence is now out of reach (no IPOs). As a result, most venture-backed companies are doomed to fail or stagger along, returning a minimal, if any, return on an initial investment. Clearly, there must be a better way to build a business.

WHAT YOU'LL LEARN FROM THIS BOOK

There is no single "right" way to start up a company. However, from my experience and the experience of others, I've learned that there are general guidelines that can improve your chances of success. Think of these guidelines like markings on a road. You don't have to follow traffic lanes to get where you want to go, but doing so increases your chances that you'll get there without wiping out in the process. Likewise, the guidelines in this book won't guarantee you success as an entrepreneur, but they can steer you away from common and easily avoidable pitfalls that could derail your company from becoming the success that it deserves.

While there are plenty of books that explain the technical details of starting a company, there are far fewer books that focus on how to make the correct strategic decisions about starting a company in the first place.

The difference between this book and others is that I'm laying out the new rules for Strategic Entrepreneurism that helped me to start up three companies and succeed with two of them. Some of my ideas may seem controversial and even counter-intuitive. But keep an open mind and I'll show you why these ideas work.

If you're thinking about starting up a company, my ideas can show you how to maximize your chance of success. If you're currently running a company, my ideas may help answer questions about why your company isn't profitable or may be struggling against its competitors.

Nobody can guarantee success, but Strategic Entrepreneurism can focus your efforts and steer you in the right direction toward making your company profitable in the shortest amount of time possible. Although I can't guarantee your company will become the next MySpace or Google, I can guarantee that my ideas will make you think about your company from a different point of view, and sometimes having the right perspective can keep you on the right side of the fine line between failure and success.

2

The Old Rules for Entrepreneurs

If you're like most people, your idea of being an entrepreneur is probably obsolete. That's not because the old ideas about being an entrepreneur were wrong. In fact, the old rules were completely right and were actually the best way to start up a company in a world where material resources made up a company's greatest assets. If you wanted to create an automobile company, you had no choice but to raise millions so that you could build a massive factory filled with equipment to create your assembly line.

The problem is that the old rules are no longer the only way to start up a company because material assets are now far less important in today's business climate than information assets. If you try to start up a company using the old rules, you'll limit your company's potential from the beginning by falling into the basic myths that trap too many entrepreneurs:

○ Waiting for massive funding to get started

○ Trying to compete against a leader

○ Trying to grow at all costs

○ Focusing solely on taking your company public through an Initial Public Offering (IPO)

MASSIVE FUNDING IS UNNECESSARY

In the old days when the strength of a company depended entirely on its material resources, you needed massive funding just to get started. Before you could even start up a construction, oil, frozen food, newspaper, or steel company, you had to invest in millions of dollars worth of equipment first. Only after you had purchased all the necessary equipment, and bought or leased the land to store everything, could you even consider running your business.

These days, the greatest resource of any corporation isn't necessarily its physical assets but its intellectual ones. Patents, trademarks, and proprietary secrets are often more valuable than machinery, real estate, or raw materials. In the old days, intellectual resources often made a product or service more valuable. Take away Coca-Cola's proprietary recipe (their intellectual resource) and you just have another company that sells carbonated beverages in bottles and cans.

In the new business climate of today, a high-tech company's intellectual resources are often the product or service itself. Imagine eBay or Amazon.com trying to run a business without their web site, or Microsoft trying to sell anything that didn't involve software. Take away Coca-Cola's secret recipe and they can still sell a product. Take away Microsoft's software or Amazon.com's web site and you don't have a business at all.

Because high-tech companies depend on intellectual assets, the start-up costs can be far lower than the costs for a non-high-tech company. Instead of buying machinery, factories, and warehouses, high-tech companies need nothing more expensive than ordinary computers and office equipment. The real cost of starting up a high-tech company relies entirely on the creativity of the entrepreneur.

Ultimately, the entrepreneur's creativity may be priceless. Low start-up costs eliminate the need for massive funding at the beginning. High-tech companies can literally be started in a garage (Hewlett-Packard), dormitory (Dell Computers), or anyplace at all. The physical location of a high-tech company doesn't matter since all you may need is a web site, which you can set up no matter where you may live. The cost of starting up a high-tech company is so low that literally anyone can do it right now.

Perhaps the greatest advantage of such low start-up costs for a high-tech company is that you don't need to rely on, or even seek, massive amounts of funding. The more funding you accept, the less control you'll have over your company. Figure 2-1 displays the different types of funding available to a startup.

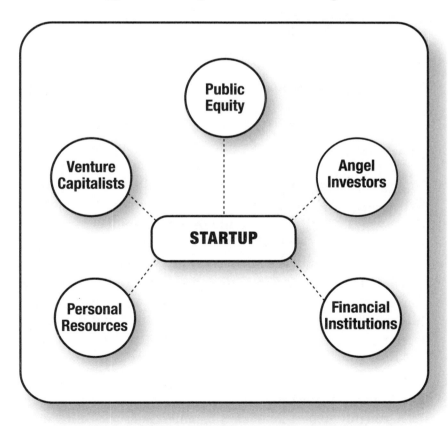

Figure 2-1. Common Sources of Funding

VENTURE CAPITALISTS
Investment firms that represent a pool of money and specializes in funding companies in exchange for equity.

ANGEL INVESTORS
Wealthy individuals who fund companies involved in fields that interest them or that they wish to promote, such as alternative energy.

PERSONAL RESOURCES
Money and assets owned by the founders of the company.

FINANCIAL INSTITUTIONS
Banks, government agencies, and private companies willing to loan money in return for interest.

PUBLIC EQUITY
Money from individuals who purchase stock in the company.

For many entrepreneurs, personal resources may be enough to start a company, but not enough to sustain it. That's why the most common type of funding comes from venture capital firms. Basically a venture capital firm looks for promising start-ups to invest in. In return for their initial start-up money, venture capital firms retain a stake in the company. The more venture capital funding used, the greater the share of the company the venture capitalists own.

By itself, accepting venture capital funding isn't bad. The problem is that venture capitalists may have their own agenda for investing in your company. In fact, it's not uncommon for venture capitalists to own so much of a company that they push out the original founders altogether. If they don't kick the original entrepreneurs out of their own company, venture capitalists can often dictate the company's direction, essentially making the founding entrepreneur practically another employee in his or her own company.

In the September 30, 2002 edition of *The Wall Street Journal*, Barnaby Federer wrote, "If you ask a VC (Venture Capitalist) what value they add, and you get them after a few drinks, they'll say, 'We replace the CEO.'"

In roughly 50 percent of all companies that succeed in raising venture capital, the founding CEO gets fired within the first year and loses all of his or her equity put into the company. This is how it usually happens.

After agreeing to fund a company, the venture capitalist seeks to put one or more additional people on the board of directors, ostensibly to add additional managerial experience. In an effort to please the venture capitalist, the entrepreneur feels obligated to agree to these changes.

These new additions to the board can now allow the venture capitalist to control the company and make wholesale management changes, which usually involves firing the founding team and replacing them with friends of the venture capitalist. This occurs not because of the founding entrepreneur's performance, but because the venture capitalist prefers having his or her friends controlling the company.

If venture capitalists don't replace the entrepreneur, the large amount of their funding makes it difficult for the company to ever make a profit. The more money venture capitalists put into a company, the less likely the founding entrepreneur will ever see a profit. For example, suppose an entrepreneur starts a company and receives $10 million dollars in venture capital funding. Now the only way this company can possibly succeed is if the company earns back the venture capitalist's original $10 million dollars.

If another company wants to buy out this company, the selling price must be higher than $10 million for the venture capitalists to make a profit. If another company buys this startup for $15 million, the venture capitalists get their original $10 million dollar investment back plus a little extra, such as $3 million dollars. The remaining money is distributed to the startup's founders, which is split among all the members of the founding team. As a general rule, the more money venture capitalists pour into your company, the less money will be left for you.

Ideally, venture capitalists want to fund the next Google or Microsoft. Since the chances of finding the next start-up block-

buster is slim, venture capitalists must invest in dozens of different companies, hoping to find the one success that can pay the
cost of backing so many startups that fail. Since venture capitalists are looking for the next big success, they'll often steer every
startup towards becoming a big company, which can actually
hurt a company's long-term prospects.

Back in 1995 Jeff Bezos founded Amazon.com as an online
bookstore. While other dot-com companies in this era grew
rapidly, prodded by venture capitalists hoping to turn their
investments into the next stock market killing, Amazon.com
grew slowly but consistently. When virtually unlimited venture
capital funding dried up during the dot-com bubble, many once
high-flying companies failed to show a profit and went out
of business. In contrast, Amazon.com's slow growth allowed
it to maintain profitability as it grew, which allowed it to
weather the dot-com bubble and still wind up making a profit
and eventually turning into the major success story that it
is today.

In their quest for massive profits as quickly as possible,
venture capitalists can often drive a company to grow faster
than its cash flow. The moment the company can't sustain this
rapid growth, it often collapses and fails. If allowed to grow
without the prodding of venture capitalists trying to get their
money out of a company as soon as possible, a startup might
grow slowly at first and then turn into a giant success like
Amazon.com.

As the dot-com bubble of the '90s proved, the more outside
funding a company accepts, the greater the disadvantages:

○ The more funding your company accepts, the
more debt it must pay back before it can return a
profit.

○ The more funding your company accepts, the less control you as the entrepreneur have in controlling the direction of your own company.

Since a high-tech company requires far less material resources, you can startup a high-tech company literally on a shoestring. Not only does this mean you can start up a company quickly and easily, but you can retain more control over your company since you can grow the company gradually at the right pace without the push from outside investors who want a quick return on their investment regardless of what's best for the company's long-term economic growth.

DEVELOPING A PRODUCT AND SEARCHING FOR A MARKET

Every business must deal with competition. Sometimes your competition is another company similar to your own, and sometimes your competition may be a business entirely different from your own. For example, movie theaters naturally compete against other movie theaters, but they also compete against video rental stores, television shows, sporting events, concerts, and any other form of entertainment that could cause customers to spend their time and money somewhere else. Sometimes your biggest competitor may be someone in an entirely different business.

Unfortunately, too many entrepreneurs believe that all you need to do is to build a better mousetrap and the world will beat a path to your door. In other words, they believe if they offer a slightly improved product, they'll gain market share. What usually happens is that if a product only offers marginal improvements, there will be no incentive for customers to switch from competing products.

Too often, entrepreneurs start up a company that competes too closely with a much larger and established rival. You may

have a better mousetrap, but you'll waste valuable resources trying to convince people that your product is superior. There can
only be one leader in any given field, and if you're not the leader,
you'll just be one of many also-rans picking up the crumbs that
the leader leaves behind.

While it's possible to knock off a leader, it's far wiser (and less
expensive) to become a leader in a new area where there is no
clearly established winner. Essentially, you need only to define a
new area of competition, but you define yourself as the new
leader in that field at the same time.

For example, no startup has the resources to compete directly
against IBM. However, back in the '80s, IBM sold mainframe
computers (hardware) so Microsoft avoided competing against
IBM's strength by selling an operating system for personal computers (software). By skirting around IBM's strength as the leader
in mainframe computers, Microsoft carved its own own niche.

Now that Microsoft is the undisputed leader of operating systems, no one would dare risk funding a startup that challenges
Microsoft's dominance in operating systems. However, other
companies are still challenging Microsoft's dominance in the
operating system market by not trying to compete head-on.

Red Hat Software doesn't rely on selling operating systems.
Instead, the company generates its revenue by selling services
for its version of the free operating system called Linux, which
is popular on server computers typically used to run networks
and web sites. Apple also doesn't try to compete against Microsoft
directly. Instead, Apple designs and controls its entire Macintosh computer. Although Apple makes its own operating system,
Apple isn't selling an operating system but a computer that just
happens to have a different operating system.

Both Red Hat Software and Apple are dominating in their
newly defined areas. Microsoft can't compete against Red Hat
Software since Red Hat gives away its operating system for
free. Microsoft also can't compete against Apple because

Microsoft sells only software while Apple sells computers. With the old rules, you were expected to build a product and compete against everyone else based on the merits of your product. In today's world, you simply cannot afford to compete against a larger, more established rival. Instead of competing directly against a rival, the key is to compete indirectly against a rival by finding your own market and establishing your leadership in that market.

STRIVING FOR RAPID GROWTH

Of course, defining a new market has its own fallacies. Many entrepreneurs believe that you need to be the first company to offer a product in a specific field. Such first-mover advantage, as it's called, essentially gives your company and product a head start against any competitors. Once you have this head start, the common belief is that you just need to grow as fast as your competitors and you'll always stay ahead.

In the old days, growth was actually necessary because the larger a company grew, the more it could take advantage of economies of scale. A car company like General Motors could buy tons of steel at a time to supply all of its factories. The more steel the company bought, the lower per unit cost. You can still see the advantage of economies of scale in traditional brick and mortar companies such as Wal-Mart or Costco. Everywhere Wal-Mart opens up a new store, they drive smaller businesses away since these smaller businesses can sell the same products, but they can't take advantage of the massive economies of scale that Wal-Mart offers.

By growing so quickly and taking advantage of their lower cost per unit on every product that they sell, companies such as Wal-Mart and Costco can undercut any competitor. In the old days, growth gave you a cost advantage while also increasing revenue, but in today's world, growth doesn't always translate into lower costs. When this occurs, you can often outgrow your resources.

Perhaps the classic example of rampant growth killing a company can be seen in the example of WebVan, which was founded back in the mid-'90s by Louis Borders, one of the co-founders of the Borders bookstore chain. The idea behind WebVan was to provide an online grocery ordering service. All you had to do was visit WebVan's web site, order the groceries you wanted, pick a time and day for delivery, and WebVan would delivery your groceries to your home within a 30-minute time frame.

As one of the first online grocery sites, WebVan tried to exploit its first-mover advantage by growing as rapidly as possible before any competitors could gain a foothold in the market. WebVan initially started in ten cities with plans to expand later into twenty-six major cities.

As part of this massive growth, WebVan rushed to create the infrastructure needed to coordinate grocery ordering and delivery. The company raised $375 million during its initial public offering and spent another $1 billion dollars to create warehouses, a fleet of delivery trucks, and an entire network of computers to track and manage their ordering and delivery system.

The problem with WebVan was that such massive growth couldn't take advantage of economies of scale. Buying groceries in bulk might have lowered costs, but the real expenses of WebVan involved running, managing, and maintaining its distribution system. The cost of running and managing one warehouse didn't drop when the company added a dozen more warehouses. Instead of costs dropping with growth, WebVan's expenses simply grew at the same rate that the company grew, but without a corresponding growth in profits as well.

After spending all this money building their infrastructure, WebVan eventually ran out of money to conduct daily operations. In their rush to expand into markets, WebVan's founders made the classic mistake of spending more money than they were bringing in. Once the company could no longer afford to maintain its day-to-day operations that were bringing in revenue, they had no choice but to declare bankruptcy soon afterwards.

In the old days, growth meant lower expenses and higher revenue. Today, growth can often mean higher expenses and lower revenue. As a result, you don't want your company to grow as rapidly as possible, but as intelligently as possible, and that could mean reigning in growth for the short-term to keep the company financially secure for the long-term.

THE BOOM OR BUST MENTALITY OF AN IPO

Since growth often equated to lower expenses and greater profits in the old days, entrepreneurs were encouraged to grow their company as fast as possible with the ultimate goal of going public and selling stock at an initial public offering (IPO). Many companies have successfully navigated the path from startup to IPO (such as eBay and Priceline.com), but for every major success story you read about, there are a hundred more companies that either failed before they could attempt an IPO or that made it to an IPO only to fail shortly afterwards.

One of the most prominent and classic IPO failures was Pets.com. This company went from going from a listing on NASDAQ where its stock peaked at $11 a share, to liquidation in nine months when its stock bottomed out at $0.19 a share. Perhaps Pets.com could have survived if it had grown slowly. Instead, the company rushed towards an IPO before it was even profitable, and burned through millions of dollars on its way to bankruptcy.

The problem isn't that so many companies fail. The problem is that so many companies fail precisely because they follow this boom or bust mentality that steers entrepreneurs into the sole option of an IPO. The truth is that not every company needs to strive for an IPO. For every successful company like

Intuit (the publishers of TurboTax and Quicken), there are probably a dozen or more private companies that are making a profit even though most people have never heard of them. A successful IPO may be the greatest validation for success that an entrepreneur can achieve, but it's not necessarily the only type of success possible.

If you focus on driving your company towards an IPO as the only option, you may never consider that you could make the same amount of money as an IPO, in much less time, by simply selling your company, or just guiding it to steady profits year after year. Given such a boom or bust mentality that only offers a single possibility when starting up a company, it's no wonder that most startups fail. If you gave a hundred people a baseball bat and gave them one chance to swing and hit a home run, most of these people would fail at the same proportion that entrepreneurs fail in taking their companies to an IPO.

REWRITING THE OLD RULES

This is the old way of starting a company: First, you obtain massive amounts of funding from venture capitalists and other investors. Second, you use this money to grow your company beyond the limited financial resources of yourself and other individuals. Third, you attempt to grow as fast and as large as possible. Once you achieve such rapid and massive growth, you take your company public and issue stock through an IPO. Then you live happily ever after. Of course, as Table 2-1 illustrates, the path to that fairy-tale ending is fraught with numerous pitfalls along the way, which increase the odds that your startup will succumb to failure.

In spite of the odds against you, such a route to success is possible, as demonstrated by numerous successful companies that appear every year. But such slavish insistence on pursuing an IPO limits your options for success. If you could find another

Old Rules Steps to Building a Startup	Failure Risk
❏ Come up with a good idea	❏ Too focused on having a unique idea with first-mover advantage. ❏ Too focused on making money and not thinking enough about solving a potential customer's problems. ❏ Attempt to create a massive, perfect company from the start rather than start small, adapt to the customers' needs, and spend as little as possible.
❏ Create founding team	❏ Add people who don't share your goals and vision for the startup. ❏ Add people who only have skills to startup a company, but don't possess skills for managing and running a company.
❏ Accept outside funding	❏ Accept too much funding too early. Risk diluting ownership of company and burdening company with debt. ❏ Misspend funding on items that won't help generate revenue.
❏ Build product	❏ Build a product that doesn't solve a customer's real needs.
❏ Market product	❏ Try to sell a product to the wrong customers because you didn't validate who might really need your product.
❏ Expand market share	❏ Try to grow as fast as possible without outside funding, without allowing profits to grow the company organically.
❏ Go through an IPO	❏ Expecting that an IPO will turn the company into a success when an IPO is just another source of outside funding.

Table 2-1. Different Ways a Startup Can Fail from Beginning to End

way to start up a company that offered you a faster, less risky path to success, while still retaining the option of achieving massive success through an IPO, you need to put the old rules for entrepreneurs aside, and focus on the new rules of Strategic Entrepreneurism that can take your startup from nothing to a million dollar success story in less time than you might think possible.

3

The New Rules for Entrepreneurs

One reason why so many startups fail is that they don't have a clear goal for what they want to achieve. If you threw a bunch of ingredients together and tossed them in the oven, you might wind up with a cake, but chances are much greater that you'd just wind up with a disgusting mess. Yet that's exactly how many entrepreneurs start up a company, and they then wonder why they fail.

The new rules for entrepreneurs are simple. Start with an end goal in mind and make that end goal to have your startup acquired by a larger company. Rather than striving for massive growth with the sole purpose of taking a company public through an IPO, you can greatly increase your chance of a profit by making your company an attractive acquisition target.

If you start up your company with the eventual goal of being acquired by another company, you immediately set the foundation for success. The basic principles are as follows:

- ○ By defining a niche for your company to dominate, you establish your company as the leader in its field without competing against more established companies that have more resources than you.

- ○ To find a niche for your company, look for a crucial problem that needs solving and then provide that solution for a Fortune 500 customer that a Fortune 100 company would want to do business with or is already doing business with.

○ By solving the problem of a Fortune 500 customer, your company will most likely be profitable as a result of this customer.

○ By developing a solution for a Fortune 500 company, you make your company a desirable acquisition target by a Fortune 100 company.

The advantage of this new, strategic approach is that you position your company for profitability and acquisition from its inception. Figure 3-1 compares the old rules of entrepreneurism with the new rules of Strategic Entrepreneurism.

BUILD YOUR COMPANY AROUND A SOLUTION FIRST

In the old days, entrepreneurs often spent years creating a product and then presented it to the world. Unfortunately, this approach means you have to create a market for your product. No matter how revolutionary your product might be, it might take years for anyone to notice, let alone to switch to your product. The problem with introducing new products is that people are often reluctant to change their old ways, even when the new product offers a clearly superior alternative.

Back in 1843 a Scottish inventor named Alexander Bain, patented a revolutionary new communication medium capable of transmitting images across distances. Nobody bought the product. In 1851 Frederick Bakewell made several improvements to Bain's invention, and still nobody bought the product, despite its clear application and obvious convenience.

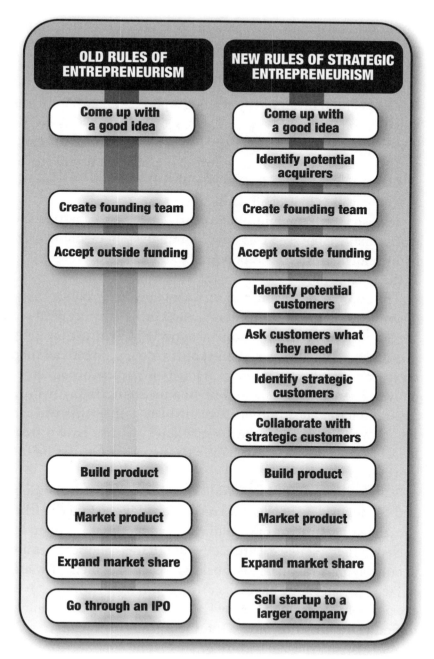

Figure 3-1. Comparing the Old and New Rules of Starting a Company

In 1861 Giovlanni Caselli sold the first machine based on this new communication medium, years before Alexander Graham Bell invented the telephone—yet sales failed to take off.

In 1924 Richard H. Ranger demonstrated the usefulness of this 80-year old invention by sending a photograph of President Calvin Coolidge from New York to London. Sales of this invention finally began, although they were often restricted to transmitting weather charts. In an effort to improve the usefulness of this invention, Herbert E. Ives modified this device to transmit colors as well as black and white images.

It wasn't until the mid 1980s, nearly 140 years later, that the world finally embraced this new communication medium, originally known as a wireless photoradiogram, but now referred to as the fax machine.

The point is that if you start up a company to introduce a new invention, or even a major improvement on an existing product, there's no guarantee that your product will ever capture any market share whatsoever. When you create a product and then try to find a market for it, you're placing the success of your company in the hands of fate and relying on hope. Unfortunately, hope can never substitute for a viable business plan. As you can see from the example of the fax machine, you may have a great idea, but you may have to wait over 100 years until the rest of the world recognizes it.

Here's a better solution: Rather than inventing a new product and spending all your time and resources trying to find a market for it, just go straight into finding a problem that needs to be solved in the first place. Ultimately, all products and services are about solving a problem. Starbucks solves the problem of wanting to enjoy an exotic blend of coffee. SouthWest Airlines solves the problem of traveling at a low-cost. Google solves the problem of finding information on the Internet.

As a startup, you can't afford to waste time creating a product and then trying to find a specific problem that it can solve. As the fax machine invention shows, sometimes your solution doesn't solve an immediate problem that anyone has.

Instead, you must find a specific problem that needs a solution right now, and then create a product specifically designed to eliminate that problem. This may not sound as sexy as creating a revolutionary new invention, but it does insure customers and cash flow when you need it the most during your initial start-up and growth phase.

Unlike the old rules of starting up a company where you create, build, and refine a prototype before unveiling it to potential customers, this new approach forces you to adapt a product to solve a customer's problem. In fact, your first customers are actually partners who help you design and modify your product until it does exactly what they want. Once you've satisfied the needs of one customer, you can satisfy the needs of similar customers and build your company one customer at a time.

PLAN TO BE ACQUIRED

When you plan for your company to be acquired from the start, every decision should be made with that goal in mind. You may not know which company may eventually want to acquire you, but you should have a general idea about which companies in a particular field may want to acquire your company and which types of companies you want to acquire your company.

With Bharosa, we created a security company, so it was only natural that other security companies would be interested in acquiring my company. However, your direct competitors aren't the only possible suitors. Since Bharosa was also a software company, other possible suitors were larger computer companies that offered services besides security, such as IBM, EMC, and Oracle.

The key is to focus on the needs of not just any customer, but on a strategic customer. By strategic, I mean that you want the type of customer that a larger company (a potential acquiring company) would want, or that a larger company already has, but to whom it would like to sell more services for greater profit and with tighter integration to keep that customer from switching to a competitor.

In Bharosa's case, the product was online security and authentication, and the strategic customer was Wells Fargo. Wells Fargo wasn't the only possible customer. In fact, it might have been easier to build the same product for a smaller bank or credit union, but the reason I chose Wells Fargo was because it was a major bank, and offered the opportunity for a big win for our company. It was like the difference between spending time trying to sell a product to a Mom and Pop store down the street, or a national chain with storefronts all over America. For the same amount of time and effort needed to make a sale, it only made sense to focus on a much larger customer such as Wells Fargo. Another advantage to partnering with Wells Fargo was that many possible acquisition suitors (IBM, EMC, Oracle, etc.) already provided services for them. By collecting Wells Fargo as Bharosa's initial customer, I set the company up as an attractive acquisition. In this case, Oracle already provided services to Wells Fargo, so by acquiring Bharosa, Oracle would then be able to provide additional security services as well. This bound Wells Fargo tighter to Oracle and insured that Wells Fargo could not easily switch services to one of Oracle's competitors since the time and effort to make the change would likely be far greater than it was worth. By choosing customers strategically from the beginning, I made Bharosa an immediate acquisition target from day one.

Even if you plan your startup around the idea of being acquired, you always have the option of continuing to grow on your own as well. Suppose Oracle (or any other company) didn't want to acquire Bharosa. In that case, Bharosa would have continued to serve Wells Fargo (and earn a steady profit), and then gradually branched out towards other banking customers and institutions that needed online security authentication, which the company did by later acquiring the United States Air Force as a customer.

Suppose we had created Bharosa without any plan other than to be acquired by another company. In that case, we might have made the classic mistake of going after growth by selling to multiple smaller banks and credit unions. This might have generated short-term growth, but it would never have created long-term security the way winning Wells Fargo as a customer did.

Too many companies make the mistake of attempting to grow without any regard for the consequences. At the time, Bharosa could have sold our products to dozens of smaller banks, or even to a larger customer such as Bank of America. The problem with expanding your customer base to include everyone is that in the short-term, it may produce instant revenue, but in the long-term, it may not help your company to grow.

If I had let Bharosa pursue the numerous smaller banks that could have used our products, we would have gained multiple customers, but would have done nothing to promote the future growth of the company. Plus our resources would have been diverted to supporting all of these multiple customers.

If I had pursued a much larger bank, such as Bank of America, I might have gained a large customer that could equal the revenue from many smaller banks. However, Bank of America lacked the reputation that Wells Fargo had as a technology leader.

Instead of pursuing Bank of America or a similar large financial institution, I made the strategic decision for Bharosa to pursue Wells Fargo, which was still a well-known company like Bank of America, but smaller. Pursuing Wells Fargo as a customer might have meant less short-term revenue, but offered a much more promising long-term future.

By pursuing Wells Fargo, I could concentrate Bharosa's limited resources on servicing the needs of one customer. Bharosa could then promote itself as a security provider on the frontier of technology by its association with Wells Fargo. This cemented Bharosa's reputation as a leader in security technology.

From a pure profit point of view, concentrating on a single customer (Wells Fargo) meant less initial revenue. However, once Bharosa proved its technology through Wells Fargo, not only were other banks eager to buy our products (which meant expending less resources to pursue new customers), but larger companies also started to view Bharosa as a serious competitor and a potential acquisition target (which I think contributed to Oracle acquiring Bharosa).

The idea of designing a startup to be acquired may seem counter-intuitive, but it greatly simplifies the path to success. You focus on selling to a strategic customer of a potential acquirer, and then you sell your company to that acquirer. If your company doesn't get acquired by another company, you still have your strategic customer to generate steady profits for your company anyway.

Compare this to a typical startup that builds a product and then tries to find a market. Such a startup needs funding to get started, then needs additional funding while it searches for a market. The longer it takes to find a market (think of the fax machine), the more additional funding it needs just to survive. Eventually, the amount of funding needed can surpass the potential profits the company could ever hope to make, and the company runs out of money and fails.

One prime example of this type of startup is Xoma, a pharmaceutical company that hasn't earned a profit since its inception in 1981. During this time, the company has churned through more than $700 million in outside funding, making it increasingly difficult for the company to ever return a profit. The moment the flow of additional funding dries up, the company will have no choice but to declare bankruptcy, taking all of its investors' money down with it.

Given the option of planning to be acquired from the start or trying to grow into a big company while relying on fate like Xoma is doing, which option do you think provides the best chance for financial success for your startup?

ALWAYS BECOME A LEADER IN YOUR FIELD

With the old rules of starting up a company, you tried to be the first to the market (first-mover advantage) because once you got started, your competitors would have to spend time and money creating the necessary material assets (warehouses, delivery trucks, manufacturing machinery, etc.) to duplicate your business and thus could never catch up.

While having a head start against a competitor may give you an initial advantage, you can't depend on such a head start to maintain your market share forever. When I formed Bharosa, there were half a dozen similar security companies already out there trying to tackle the same market that Bharosa was targeting. The difference between Bharosa and our competitors was Bharosa's implementation of our solution.

In the field of online security authentication, the common solution relied on hardware devices, such as ID cards, biometrics (fingerprint readers), or other physical devices that people needed to carry or use. Bharosa could have introduced a similar hardware security authentication product, but that would have set the company up as just another me-too company in a field already crowded with competitors.

Instead, Bharosa offered one of the first software-only security authentication products. Not only did this avoid the hassle and expense of buying and using hardware security devices, but it also separated Bharosa from all of its competitors. If you wanted a hardware solution, you had to choose from half a dozen different companies. If you wanted a software solution, the best choice at the time was Bharosa.

Bharosa never became a leader in the security field, but it did become a leader in the software-only security authentication field. As long as you're the leader in any field, you'll be an attractive option to potential customers.

ACCEPT FUNDING RELUCTANTLY

Initially, every startup is funded by the entrepreneur's own assets and the resources of the entrepreneur's team. (Steve Jobs and Steve Wozniak initially formed Apple by selling Steve Jobs' VW microbus and Steve Wozniak's Hewlett-Packard calculator.) However, no matter how much money the entrepreneur and his or her friends and family can raise, it will likely never be enough to grow the company beyond its initial phase. At this point, outside funding may be necessary.

The biggest threat of outside funding is that the more money you accept from outsiders, the more you'll have to share ownership and control of your company with others. Accept too much outside funding and you risk not only sinking your company in debt, but losing control and ownership of your company altogether.

The reason this happens is that the primary source of outside funding comes from venture capital firms, whose primary goal is to fund the next success story such as Google or Amazon. Since the chance of funding the next major success story is slim, venture capital firms typically fund multiple startups. The idea is that out of ten startups, roughly nine will fail while one will succeed and make enough of a profit to cover the losses of the other nine failed companies—and then some.

As a result, venture capitalists can't afford to let any of their investments become anything except a major success. Traditionally, startups can make money by either growing as a private company, being acquired by another company, or going public through an IPO.

From an entrepreneur's point of view, all three possibilities offer a hefty profit, but from a venture capitalist's point of view the only acceptable option is to at least plan to take a company public through an IPO. To accomplish this task venture capitalists often push a company to grow as fast as possible, even if it's not in the best interests to do so at the moment.

Once in control, venture capitalists will typically spurn slow growth and the possibility of merging with another company simply because neither option offers a hefty return on their investment in a short amount of time. Ultimately the problem isn't necessarily the acceptance of funding from the venture capitalists, but in accepting funding from venture capitalists who have different goals from your own. Where one venture capitalist may allow a company to grow organically, another venture capitalist may push a company towards an IPO too quickly before the company can create a solid foundation for itself. The lesson is that if you're going to accept funding from venture capitalists, choose your venture capitalists with care.

The traditional business model of venture capitalists is fast becoming obsolete and the smart venture capitalists know it. Despite the vast amounts of money they represent, venture capitalists still invest in horrible business models, and then they wonder why they lose money on so many of their investments.

Ever heard of DigiScents? The venture capitalists did, and they funded it to the tune of $20 million before the company folded. The business model of DigiScents focused on transmitting smells over the Internet. If this sounds like a solution for solving a critical problem that people would be willing to pay for, then I have a bridge in Brooklyn I'd like to sell you.

Besides making poor investment decisions, the venture capital industry is facing a more serious dilemma. Most senior venture capitalists are retiring, allowing a fresh crop of unseasoned venture capitalists to run the profession. If you think venture capitalists are making poor decisions today, wait until these inexperienced venture capitalists start making the mistakes that more experienced venture capitalists have recognized and avoided for a long time.

With the low cost of starting up a company and the growing distrust of entrepreneurs toward venture capitalists, many companies are actually turning venture capital away and opting to grow more slowly through their own earnings, or by accepting funding from non-venture capitalists. One of the more popular forms of outside funding comes from individuals known as angel investors.

An angel investor is often a wealthy individual who invests in startups partly for the potential profits and equity stake in the company, and partly because he or she believes in the company, the entrepreneur, or the company's products. For example, many electric car, alternative energy, and environmental friendly companies receive funding from an angel investor who wants to support companies pursuing activities in that particular field.

Both venture capitalists and angel investors want a quick return on their investment, but angel investors use their own money as opposed to a pool of money from other investors. Often angel investors are former executives or entrepreneurs themselves, so they can offer their guidance in steering a company towards profitability.

Given a choice, it's almost always best to accept as little outside funding as possible and to grow your company organically through its own natural growth. Since that's not always possible, the next best source of funding comes from angel investors and venture capitalists willing to accept a profit without necessarily forcing your company to go through an IPO.

Remember, any time you borrow money, not only do you have to pay it back, but you may also find certain strings attached to this money. As a general rule, the more outside funding you accept, the less control you'll have over your company and the lower your financial stake in that company. The old rules told entrepreneurs to accept outside funding to make the company grow. The new rules tell you to keep outside funding to a minimum so that you retain as much control and equity in your company as possible.

PRACTICING STRATEGIC ENTREPRENEURISM

The idea behind Strategic Entrepreneurism is to know your desired outcome and then to focus all your efforts to achieve that desired outcome. If you don't know where you want your company to go, you probably will never get there.

The first part of Strategic Entrepreneurism is finding an urgent problem that needs solving and then finding a solution to that problem. This defines your company's product or service.

The second part of Strategic Entrepreneurism involves deciding which types of companies may be interested and capable of acquiring your own company. Find out the most important customers that these potential suitors have in common. This defines the specific customer you should target for your own company.

Finally, concentrate your resources on solving a pressing problem (using your product or service) for this strategic customer. This immediately gives your company an immediate source of income along with the credibility to attract additional customers and potential suitors at the same time.

Without Strategic Entrepreneurism, you can waste time creating a product or service that people don't really need. By lacking focus on who a strategic customer might be, you may further waste time and resources pursuing customers who can't help you attract additional customers or the interest of potential suitors.

Without the guidance and focus of Strategic Entrepreneurism, you risk leaving your company's fate to chance. With Strategic Entrepreneurism, every decision brings you one step closer to your eventual goal of being acquired by another company. When another company finally acquires your company and you walk away with a hefty payout, others will think you were just lucky. But you will know the real reason for your success. Best of all, you'll know exactly how to duplicate your success with another startup.

Given a choice between following the old rules of entrepreneurism or the new rules, which choice do you think gives you the most flexibility and increases your chance of earning a massive financial reward at the same time?

	Old Rules	**New Rules**
Product	❏ Create a product first and then search for a market.	❏ Find a customer with a problem first and then build a solution.
Startup Goal	❏ Grow as fast as possible to reach an IPO.	❏ Grow as fast as possible to become an attractive acquisition target.
Market Share	❏ Fight to become a leader in your market.	❏ Create a new market and definte your company as the leader.
Outside Funding	❏ Accept as much funding as possible to grow.	❏ Accept as little funding as possible to grow organically.
Possible End Results	❏ Success: Company issues IPO and becomes a dominant leader in its field.	❏ Success: Company gets acquired by a larger company.
	❏ Company requires ad-ditional funding, increasing debt and diluting ownership.	❏ Success: Company funds its growth through increasing profits.
	❏ Company fails.	❏ Company fails.

Table 3-1. Comparison of Old and New Rules of Entrepreneurism

4

Strategically Designing Your Company for Success

In the enterprise software industry eighty percent of the market (and profits) go to a handful of companies while thousands of other companies fight over the remaining twenty percent. A new startup in this market could challenge one of the three leaders, but the odds are that the startup wouldn't survive in direct competition.

While such dismal odds might discourage anyone from starting up a company in the enterprise software industry, the fact is that every industry has its handful of dominant leaders with many smaller companies scrambling for the remaining crumbs left behind. If you want your company to survive, you must design it from its inception to survive in such a hostile environment, and the best way to do this is through strategic design.

The main focus of strategic design is to make your company an attractive acquisition target. Accordingly, entrepreneurs setting up their companies for future acquisition must begin by strategically selecting customers who can attract potential acquirers. They must also consider every other aspect of the start-up—from its team, to its technology, to its concepts, to its contracts—not just for its stand-alone business value, but for its attractiveness to an acquirer. The more attractive you make your company to a larger one, the more likely your company will not only survive, but thrive and make a handsome profit.

STARTING UP A COMPANY

Startups typically go through three distinct phases. In Phase I, a startup is scrambling just to gather enough resources to open its doors for business, whether that means leasing physical office space, testing and refining a product, or just putting up a web site. This initial phase is most crucial since it lays the foundation for the future success (or failure) of the company.

In Phase II, a company begins its initial growth. This is the time when a company's resources are typically focused on marketing and sales of its product or services. No matter how fast (or slowly) a company grows, it eventually reaches a plateau. This can occur due to the limited number of customers the company's sales force can reach or because the market for the company's product eventually gets saturated.

In Phase III, the company starts scaling, which is a larger form of growth. Instead of just growing by adding new customers, scaling occurs when a company enters new markets. For example, a company may initially grow within the East coast of the United States and then later expand to the rest of the country. Then it might scale up even further by expanding from the United States to branch out into international markets.

Another form of scaling might occur when a company introduces new products or services to an existing market. For example, a company might start out by selling anti-virus software and then scale up by introducing intrusion detection software and anti-spam software to expand its presence in its existing markets. The same company could also scale up by selling its products to the enterprise and business market, and then branch out to selling to the consumer market (or vice versa).

In designing your company strategically, Phases I and II are the most crucial. In Phase I, you must start with a product or service that can be attractive to a potential acquiring company. In Phase II, you must focus your limited resources on attracting the types of customers a potential acquiring company might want. Do these correctly and you may not even need to worry about Phase III since that's when another company may acquire your company. If another company doesn't acquire your startup, then your company will already be primed for growth in Phase III anyway.

PHASE I: PUTTING YOUR COMPANY TOGETHER STRATEGICALLY

As the entrepreneur your first job is to create a product or service, and then to create a company that can provide that product or service. No matter what your product or service may be, the most important step is that the entrepreneur, or someone on your team, must be capable of creating that product or service.

If you're more of a business person but want to sell a high-tech product, someone else on your team needs to be the engineer, scientist, or programmer who can create that product. If you're the inventor or creator of a product, then you need a business person as part of your team. An entrepreneur may be the leader of a company, but he or she always needs the help of other people to succeed. In many cases the difference between a small, local company and a big, national company is nothing more than that the big, national company planned to become big from the start.

Although the entrepreneur may be the leader, few companies can survive without a team of supporting people who bring unique skills or experience to the company. The size of your team is less important then the qualities it brings to the company. While every company needs accountants, lawyers, and marketers, these services aren't absolutely crucial in creating and designing your product. Your start-up team should consist only of those people whose resources and skills your company absolutely needs to survive.

The number and types of people on an entrepreneur's team will vary depending on the company and its product. If you're starting up an Internet business that only requires a web site, you can often be a one-person company. If you're starting up a biofuel or robotics company, you'll likely need more people than yourself. As a general rule, the smaller the team, the more nimble and flexible it will be. Like a baseball team where every player has a definite purpose, an entrepreneur's team must consist of the minimum number of people who all have a definite purpose in starting up a company and making it profitable as quickly as possible.

Ideally, each person on your team should provide two types of resources: First, that person's skills or experience should help the company get started; second, that person should also offer contacts or skills that would help make your company attractive to a potential suitor.

For example, your company may need someone with sales experience in the e-commerce field. Since you can find many people who have similar sales experience, you also want to choose someone who can not only help your company get started, but can also help guide your company towards the eventual goal of being acquired.

If you're designing your company to be acquired by Google or Microsoft, you might want someone who has both sales experience in e-commerce and contacts or previous working experience with Google or Microsoft. Additionally, Google or Microsoft will find it less risky to integrate former employees. Ideally, every member of your team can help your company get started and get acquired.

After assembling your team the first year of your company is typically spent in the research and development phase. This is the time to strategically position your company's product to solve a pressing problem for a customer that a larger company might find attractive.

First, your company's products should not be created in a vacuum. In other words, your company's products must be created in collaboration with a major customer. This insures that you'll have a product immediately that you can sell to generate revenue, and that you'll have a customer who can't switch to a rival easily since they'll have invested their own time helping you customize a solution just for them.

Second, your startup's product shouldn't compete directly with a larger company, but should complement that larger company's product. For example, suppose your company sells tax preparation software. Your startup would directly compete against another company that sells similar tax preparation software, but it might appeal to a different company that only sells financial planning software.

Third, sometimes your product is less important to a potential suitor than the customers you have. For example, your startup might specialize in selling drones and miniature robots to the military. A defense contractor might not necessarily want to expand into robotics, but it would definitely be interested in having yet another product to sell to its existing military customers. By providing additional products to sell to the same customers, a larger company can tie customers to them so completely that it would be nearly impossible for a competitor to steal these customers away.

Finally, your products may not be of particular interest to a suitor, but the technology behind your products may actually be the most attractive feature. For example, you might have an electric car company, which might catch the eye of a robotics company. The robotics company may not necessarily care about electric cars, but they might care about the battery technology your company possesses that could make their own products more useful and valuable as a result.

Your products and your customers are more than just a way to make money. When used strategically both your products and your customers can be crucial to attracting a potential suitor. At the end of Phase I your company should lay the foundation to attract a potential acquirer by developing:

○ A product or service that complements a larger company's current offerings

○ A product or service in a market that complements a larger company's market share

○ An entrepreneurial team who can create and nurture a startup, and offer skills and experience that a potential acquirer might want

If you don't design your company towards the future goal of being acquired, these are some of the possible pitfalls:

○ Your company tries to compete against the market leaders, head-on. Since the market leaders have more resources, they can wear down your company in a war of attrition that a small startup will likely never win. End result: Your venture fails.

○ Your company creates a product first and then looks for a market. End result: You waste time and money searching for customers. If you're lucky, you'll find enough customers for your product and survive. If you're unlucky, your company will fail.

○ Your company enters or creates a market where there are no large, established leaders. Your company can thrive until new competitors appear, but being first doesn't always translate into assured success. End result: Your company becomes one of many struggling to survive and establish itself against numerous competitors.

○ You put together an entrepreneurial team designed to start up your company. Once your company starts up, the company may lack a clear focus and direction on how to grow. The people on your team may have been perfect to start up a company, but not ideal for growing a company to be acquired. End result: The company wastes time and resources pursuing the wrong customers or growing too fast.

PHASE II: GROWING A STARTUP

Initially, every startup begins with zero assets, no profits, few resources and perhaps a handful of people, possibly even just the entrepreneurs. By the second year the company should have grown through sales of its products or services, and increased the number of employees, in addition to the original founders.

At this point the company should focus all of its resources on snaring a strategic customer, which is the best customer that can make the company an attractive acquisition. A big mistake entrepreneurs make at this early stage is to try to grab any customers just for the potential revenue. In the short-term this generates cash flow, but in the long-term it does little to help your company distinguish itself from any competitors. You don't just want any customer; you want the type of customer who can help establish your company as the leader in its field.

For example, suppose your company sells solar panels. You could sell solar panels to individual homeowners, but the problem with this approach is that you'd waste time trying to sell to multiple customers. Selling to one homeowner does little to increase the chance of selling to a second homeowner.

To provide the greatest amount of profit while expending the least amount of effort, it's usually best to focus your product or service toward other businesses rather than toward individuals. Rather than expending time and energy making sales to multiple individuals, you can earn that same amount in less time by selling to a single company.

Besides making more money per sale to businesses rather than individuals, there's another reason why selling to businesses is more strategic. When you sell anything to a business, you can associate your company with that business.

For example, suppose you sold solar panels to Whole Foods Markets. Because so many people think of Whole Foods Market as an environmentally-friendly company, earning Whole Foods Market as a customer would also associate your own company an environmentally-friendly brand. Once people associate your company with a better-known company, such as Whole Foods Market, future potential customers will likely apply Whole Foods Market's values to your own company. So strategically selecting your customers lets you earn money while associating your company with the reputation of another one. Such association is nothing more than a form of free and continuous advertising that establishes your company as a leader in its field.

A customer should earn your company a profit, enhance your company's reputation, and provide a potential acquiring company with access to a new customer or a new product to sell to an existing customer. Sound like a lot to expect from a customer? It is—which is why you must pick and choose your customers strategically. The biggest mistake is to look for the customer who can generate the most revenue. The real solution is to look for the customer who can help your company to be acquired.

Suppose your company sells electric cars. You might think a bigger car company, such as Ford Motors or Toyota, might be a natural company to acquire your own. That may not be the case when an electric car directly challenges their current business. Instead, the best potential acquirer might be a company that could benefit from greater electricity usage, such as General Electric.

Whatever company you believe might be interested in acquiring your company, look for the type of customer that would best benefit that company. If you decide that General Electric might be interested in acquiring your electric car company, ask yourself what type of customer you could get that would be the type of customer that General Electric might want.

Perhaps concentrate on selling your first fleet of electric cars to a delivery service such as the post office or Federal Express. Would General Electric want this type of customer? Maybe, but if they do, they might see acquiring your electric car company as one way to grab one of these customers.

While you can never be sure which company might want to acquire your own, or what type of customers they want for themselves, you can make educated guesses based on the types of companies a larger company has acquired in the past and the types of customers they have gathered. While you may never know if selling a fleet of electric cars to UPS or Federal Express will help make your electric car company attractive to a larger company, you can be certain that if you focus on selling electric cars to individuals or smaller businesses such as retirement homes or golf courses, you may make a profit, but your customers won't be as attractive to a major corporation.

What makes companies an attractive acquisition target isn't just their technology or product, but their current customer base. If your company's customers consist only of individuals or small businesses such as local restaurants or dry cleaners, but a competing company with a similar product (or even an inferior one) has major corporate customers, it may be more attractive to the company in a position to acquire one of you. Ultimately, you are the one who can pick your customers, so choose them wisely.

PHASE III: SCALING OR SELLING A STARTUP

In the first year a startup struggles just to survive. In the second year a startup makes its first sales and starts to grow. By the third year, a startup should be stable and ready to expand, which is known as scaling up a company. As a general rule of thumb, startups in their third year typically have assets up to $10 million with less than 120 employees.

This is the time when a company has two options that it can pursue simultaneously. First, the company can continue to grow, gaining more strategic customers and increasing its revenue. Second, a company can search for suitors who may be interested in buying out the startup. This does not mean hanging a "for sale" sign on your company's front door. Searching for and attracting possible suitors must be a deliberate process.

Since your company can continue to grow while also looking for a buyer, by actively searching for an acquirer you essentially double your chances of profitability. If a company wants to acquire your startup, you can cash out. If no company wants to acquire your startup, you can continue growing and increasing revenue. This puts you in a no-lose situation.

Now compare this situation with a similar startup that didn't plan to be acquired from its inception. Such a startup might have spent time and money pursuing all kinds of customers who may not be of interest to a larger suitor. In this situation, the startup may have no other choice but to continue to grow. If this is no longer possible, then the startup may find itself in financial trouble without the possibility of an acquisition to save it. Given these two choices, which position would you want to be in?

STRATEGIC STARTUPS

If you're going to start up a company, do it with the end goal in mind which is to be acquired by a larger corporation. You may not need or want to be acquired, but having this option available is preferable to not having this option at all.

During Phase I and II of putting your company together:

○ Create your team with the fewest people possible where each person is absolutely necessary for your startup to succeed.

○ Put people on your team who can both help your startup in the beginning and increase your startup's appeal to a potential suitor.

○ Create a product with the collaboration of a strategic customer

○ Create a product that could complement a larger company's current product line

○ Target customers that are current customers of a larger company or desirable customers for a larger company

By the time your company reaches Phase III, your initial strategy will have made your company both an attractive acquisition target and a profitable and stable company that could continue to grow and thrive on its own if necessary. When you design your company strategically, you minimize the effects of chance and maximize your probability for success. That sets your startup on the path to profitability no matter what industry you may be in.

	Old Rules	**New Rules**
Customers	❒ Go for quantity. Get as many customers as possible for maximum growth and revenue.	❒ Go for quality. Get the customers that will help you design your product, has a reputation that can help you sell to other customers, and is the type of customer a larger company would like as their own customer.
Company Team	❒ Get the best people you can find to help you run the company.	❒ Get the best people you can find to help you run the company, create the product and establish contacts with potential acquiring companies.
Competition	❒ Compete directly against larger rivals and rely on product superiority to succeed.	❒ Carve out a niche that larger rivals are missing and establish yourself as the leader in this niche. Design your product to complement, not compete, against a larger rival.
Long-Term Goal	❒ Become the dominant leader in the market.	❒ Become an attractive acquisition target.
		❒ Become a dominant leader in a niche market, capable of growing and becoming a dominant leader in a larger market.

Table 4-1. Comparison of Old and New Rules of Entrepreneurism

5

Finding the Right Business Idea: The Search for the Not-So Holy Grail

Every company begins with an idea. This idea defines a company's purpose, which indirectly also defines the solution that the company offers. For example, the idea behind eBay was to offer auctions over the Internet. The idea behind Priceline.com was to let people establish their own prices to pay for items such as airline tickets.

To be profitable a successful idea must solve a pressing need for a large number of people. Although an idea can lay the foundation for a company, it's not necessarily the crucial factor for success.

Perhaps the biggest myth of too many entrepreneurs is the belief that success relies on having a unique idea that nobody else has ever thought of. Unfortunately, if you have such an unusual idea that nobody has ever considered it, chances are good that you'll have a hard time marketing it. Potential customers may not understand how your product can solve their most urgent problems. Or even worse, they may simply be reluctant to change their habits to adopt your solution.

At one time people used to shop at markets by holding a basket in their hands. The basket limited the number of items any single person could comfortably carry and hold. When Sylvan Goldman invented the shopping cart in 1937 for Piggly-Wiggly Markets, nobody wanted to use shopping carts even though they could see that shopping carts made it easier to carry more and larger items without strain. Men considered shopping carts effeminate and women complained that shopping carts looked too much like baby carriages. It was only after Mr. Goldman hired models to demonstrate how to use shopping carts in actual markets that people finally saw the advantages of using them. If Mr. Goldman had failed to do this, there's a good chance that nobody would have seen the benefit of shopping carts and this invention would have withered away, despite its obvious usefulness.

The truth is that a unique idea by itself won't necessarily carry a company to instant success. If you focus your entire startup on the belief that you need a unique idea, you'll be in for a surprise. Take any idea, search for it on the Internet, and you'll probably find half a dozen other people with similar ideas. Their solutions might be implemented differently, but they may be closer to your own idea than you like.

Everyone has a good idea. Even some of the biggest failures, such as Pets.com (an online pet supply store) started off as a good idea. Since a good idea alone can't sustain a company, the real key is to find the right idea and then find the right way to implement that idea profitably.

The fact that half a dozen (or more) people have the same idea simply validates that you have a good idea in the first place. If you're truly the only one with a unique idea, chances are good that you're the only one with that idea because nobody else thinks that idea will work.

One reason why entrepreneurs believe they need a unique idea is that they think such an unusual idea will give them "first-mover" advantage. This means if you're the first company in a particular field, you can become the dominant leader by default.

While this first-mover advantage is certainly helpful, it can't sustain a company in the long-term. Being first into the market may give you a head start on your competition, but it could also mean you're paving the way to make it easier for competitors to follow and eventually to catch up and pass you.

In the early days of the personal computer industry, Microsoft was a small company while a much larger company (called Digital Research) had the first-mover advantage in cornering the personal computer operating system market. The only reason that Microsoft surpassed Digital Research was that the market abruptly changed.

When IBM decided to enter the personal computer market, they needed an operating system for their computers. IBM initially approached Digital Research, but failed to reach an agreement. After being rebuffed by the market leader (Digital Research), IBM had no choice but to look for a solution from one of Digital Research's many competitors, one of which happened to be Microsoft. Since Digital Research was slow to respond to changing market conditions, Microsoft took advantage and blossomed into a billion dollar organization.

If you base the success of your company just around an idea itself, you'll probably waste time and money trying to develop a market for your idea. If you think having a great idea will give you first-mover advantage, you better have a plan to keep you in the dominant position because you could otherwise lose this lead. To succeed as an entrepreneur, you can't rely only on a unique idea that nobody else has, nor can you rely only on a unique idea to give you a first-mover advantage. What you need is a good idea that you can also implement strategically.

LOOK FOR THE HOLY GRAIL

An idea is only as important as the problem that it solves. The more important and difficult the problem is, the better the chance for profitability. If your idea solves a trivial problem or a problem for a small number of people, you may only have an idea for a small business. If your idea can solve an important problem or a problem for a large number of people, you'll have the market necessary to create a large corporation.

The most important part of any idea is whether it solves the type of problem that I dub a Holy Grail. Like the myth surrounding the Holy Grail, an entrepreneur's Holy Grail should be a problem that's seemingly impossible to achieve. If you can solve a seemingly impossible problem, you can be sure you'll have a large enough market for your product.

Think of the idea behind FedEx. Before FedEx appeared most businesses and people relied on the postal system, which didn't always give the speediest service. So the Holy Grail of document and package delivery was to deliver something as fast as possible, approaching the speed of instantaneously. While FedEx can't deliver instantaneously, it can guarantee delivery overnight, which is fast enough for most purposes. This solution isn't the Holy Grail, but it comes much closer to this ideal than the post office.

Every field has its own Holy Grails. In the alternate energy field, the Holy Grail is to produce more energy at less cost than traditional energy sources. In the pharmaceutical industry, the Holy Grail is to invent or discover a drug that can cure life-threatening diseases such as cancer and AIDS. In the computer industry, the Holy Grail is to create a lightweight, laptop computer that offers all the features of a desktop computer while running for days at a time off battery power.

If you have an idea for a company, ask yourself if it solves a Holy Grail type of problem. Every industry has its own Holy Grails. Most of them are impossible, but the closer you get to solving a seemingly impossible problem, the more potential profit your idea can generate. You can make money solving less important problems in any industry, but looking for the Holy

Grail of problems steers you faster toward a stronger product and ultimately a more attractive company to potential suitors.

USE THE NOT-SO HOLY GRAIL

By its nature a Holy Grail problem is extremely difficult, if not impossible, to solve. So rather than trying to solve the impossible, you simply need to try to solve the possible. That means identifying an existing Holy Grail problem and applying current solutions to that problem in a unique and creative way, which I call a not-so Holy Grail.

In the case of Bharosa, the Holy Grail was solving the problem of authentication. If someone connects to a web site over the Internet, how can you verify that the person logging in is authorized to access that web site?

Previous solutions to this Holy Grail problem involved additional hardware, such as requiring users to carry an ID token or log in to a computer using a fingerprint. The theory was that only authorized users would possess the necessary ID token or valid fingerprint. Un-

As an entrepreneur, you must first identify what a Holy Grail problem might be, and then create a solution to solve this problem as elegantly and completely as possible. Some Holy Grail problems in different industries include:

SEARCH – Create a new way to rank search results that includes content and visuals. Generate enterprise revenue beyond advertising.

RETAIL – Build/ship products completely online including cars, clothes, food, etc.

GREEN TECH – Provide one quantifiable standard for corporate green rating.

FINANCE – Develop a single portal/single sign-on for all online vendor accounts.

SECURITY – Create a product that connects all disparate vendor products recently installed in enterprise.

Obviously these are just a handful of Holy Grail problems but they should get your mind to thinking about how your solution can best solve a Holy Grail problem in your particular field.

fortunately, such hardware measures made the computer clumsier to use. If an authorized user lost the ID token, then the computer would lock that person out.

Employing passwords offers an alternative to such hardware measures. The problem with passwords is that they can be easily stolen, especially if someone peeks over your shoulder as you type your password in. Trying to solve this Holy Grail problem meant using a variety of solutions, none of which were practical for everyday use.

That's the market that Bharosa targeted, and solved the password problem by essentially incorporating the hardware authentication features entirely in software.

In the authentication industry, one Holy Grail is a method whereby a user enters a password securely right in front of a hacker. The hacker literally watches the computer keyboard and screen but cannot decipher what is being entered. At Bharosa, we invented the Virtual Keyboard and Slider interfaces, which was part of our Authenticator software that enabled secure password entry that was stronger than what existed on the market at that time. Essentially, all a hacker could see was a turning wheel, a virtual keyboard, or a slider as the user entered password characters as shown in Figure 5-1. However, the solution, like all security solutions, had vulnerabilities and therefore was not the Holy Grail.

Another Holy Grail in the authentication industry is a strong security solution (e.g. smart card, one-time-password generating or biometric solution) that millions of users can easily adopt and use. If a hacker steals the online password, the theory goes, the password will change 60 seconds later and/or the hacker will also need a smart card or gadget for access that are very difficult to steal. These are strong security solutions but not good practical solutions for many users because of the high logistics costs and complexity. Bharosa's Tracker program turned the computer, something already in the user's possession, into the smart

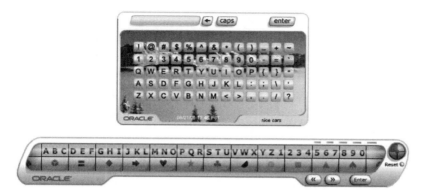

Figure 5-1. The Virtual Keyboard and Slider Interface

card or gadget by tracking IP address and other characteristics unique to the computer and therefore the user. The only way a hacker could get access would be by physically gaining access to the computer as well.

Verisign, Vasco, and Entrust as well as a slew of privately held competitors searched for both Holy Grails in the authentication market. For a time, Bharosa was the only company that deployed both an Authenticator-like and a Tracker-like solution under one roof. That was one of the factors that led to significant customer wins that included Wells Fargo.

A Holy Grail problem is nearly impossible to solve, but a not-so Holy Grail solution is possible to create: Just use existing technology to improve or tweak an existing application. Everyone has already found partial solutions to a Holy Grail problem. Your idea just needs to improve on an existing solution to make it less expensive, faster, easier to use, or more convenient. A not-so Holy Grail doesn't need to make massive improvements to solve a problem, but just needs to make incremental ones. In a sense, a not-so Holy Grail solution gives you a first-mover advantage since you're carving out a niche within an existing field.

Normally a niche might seem to limit your company to the fringes, but by tackling a Holy Grail type of problem, your solution will create a dominant position since you'll have much less competition. This allows you to compete against larger companies simply because they won't have an equivalent product to compete against you. (This also makes your company attractive as an acquisition target for a larger company too.)

A not-so Holy Grail solution frees you from falling into the typical traps of a novice entrepreneur:

○ You don't need to create an idea that nobody has ever thought of. In fact, you need to tackle a problem that almost everyone has thought about before—but just doesn't know the best way to solve.

○ You don't need to rely on first-mover advantage since your solution literally creates that for you from its inception. You just need to solve a current problem using existing technology, applied in a creative way.

○ You don't need to waste time marketing and selling your product since targeting a Holy Grail type of problem immediately assures that your company and product will be accepted and profitable.

COLLABORATING WITH A STRATEGIC CUSTOMER

Most entrepreneurs rush to create a product and then waste time trying to find a market for their product. Even worse, you could create a product that isn't quite what a customer wants, which means you'll need to waste more time and money redesigning your product to fit the market needs. Essentially, designing a product before knowing your market is just an expensive and time-consuming form of guessing. It's possible to spend millions creating the wrong product, and then have to spend more money designing the right one.

A better solution is to go straight to your potential customers to ask what they really need. Collaborating with a customer not only helps you create a product that's exactly what someone wants, but it also strengthens your company's relationship with that customer. After all, if you spent six months to a year customizing a solution for a customer, what are the odds that customer would ever want to leave you for a competitor's product?

Collaborating with your customers helps you design a product right the first time and helps you build your customer base before your product is even ready. Your customer literally helps shape your product as you create it.

Your customer understands the Holy Grail type of problem better than you do, and can validate whether your not-so Holy Grail solution is practical and desirable. Because of this collaboration, your customer essentially becomes your partner in helping you create the best product possible.

When you collaborate with a customer, you can choose any type of customer, so choose one for strategic reasons. For example, if your company is developing software to make printing more efficient over the Internet, would you rather have a local printing shop as a customer or the nationally recognized Kinko's chain? If you have a product that can convert used vegetable oil into biofuel, would you rather have a local diner as a customer or McDonald's with its international reputation?

Choosing a strategic customer for collaboration offers several benefits. First, you gain the experience of a large company. Having a local printer test out your product may result in a product that works only for that particular business. However, having a national printing chain like Kinko's test your product will be likely to result in a field-tested product that can be transferred and used in other large corporations just as easily.

Besides gaining the experience of a larger corporation, another reason to choose your customers strategically is to enhance the reputation of your own company and product in comparison. Having a product that solves the problem of your local diner is less impressive than having the same product that solves the problem of McDonald's.

You may have the best product in the world, but having a local restaurant as a customer will never be as impressive as having an international restaurant chain as a customer. By choosing a customer that already has a reputation, your product and company can use this customer's reputation to boost your own credibility and attract additional customers.

A third reason to choose your customers strategically boils down to money. If you customize a product for a particular customer, you link that customer to your company in ways that a competitor can never do. Choose a large customer and that one customer alone could generate enough revenue to keep your company profitable. Since one of the biggest problems of start-ups is running out of money, grabbing a high-paying customer early guarantees your cash flow and profits.

A final reason to choose your customers strategically is to look ahead to the type of customers that a potential suitor might want. If your company has developed a less expensive and more efficient way to turn salt water into drinking water, you could market your product to fishing fleets, but a more strategic customer might be cruise lines or even the United States Navy. Getting the United States Navy as a customer will make your company more attractive to potential suitors, especially if those suitors already sell, or wish to sell, products or services to the United States Navy.

If another company buys out your company, they'll inherit the United States Navy as a customer as well. Since gaining new customers is much more difficult than retaining existing customers, your acquisition of another company can often be worthwhile just for the expanded customer base the company that buys you will receive. By grabbing high-profile customers to help you create and fine-tune your product, your company will be valuable both for its product and for its customer base.

Compare this strategic targeting of customers with the way most entrepreneurs behave:

○ They don't collaborate on the development of their product with a customer. End result: Creating a product that nobody wants or needs.

○ They don't collaborate with a customer that's representative of the target industry. End result: The customized product may only solve a narrow problem that can't be easily adapted for others. Now you'll need to spend time and money redesigning your product.

○ They collaborate with any customers who are convenient. End result: The customer base simply generates revenue, but doesn't help attract additional customers or attract a potential suitor.

○ They collaborate with a large customer without considering the strategic importance of this customer to a potential suitor. End result: A potential suitor may decide to avoid acquiring your company since you don't have a customer base that the acquiring company might want.

A customer is more than just a source of income. The right customer can help you design your product, test your product so you can market it to others, provide you with a steady cash flow, help you attract more customers based on the reputation of your existing customers, and help you attract a suitor who wants your customer base.

Taking the time to strategically choose your customers may seem like a lot of work, but the final result is to strengthen your company's position in the market while ensuring profitability. Ultimately, your company's value lies with its customer base. A handful of strategic customers is far preferable to a dozen or more less strategic customers.

Ideally, every customer should be a source of income, a collaborator for improving your product, a reference to help you attract new customers, and an asset for attracting potential suitors. This may ask a lot from your customers, but by choosing your customers wisely, you'll increase the odds that your company will grow and survive in the long-term. Given this choice, you literally cannot afford not to choose your customers strategically.

TESTING YOUR OWN IDEA

Before you commit a company into building and supporting your idea, take a few moments to make sure your idea meets the criteria for Strategic Entrepreneurism. If you answer no to any of the following questions, you might want to rethink and modify your idea.

- ○ Does your idea solve a Holy Grail type of problem? (This insures that your solution will be eagerly adopted by others and increases the chance of greater customer collaboration.)

- ○ Is your idea a creative use of existing technology (a not-so Holy Grail solution)? (This insures that your product can be created.)

- ○ Are other companies trying to solve the same problem? (This verifies that a solution to this problem will likely be profitable.)

○ Can you collaborate with a customer to refine and develop a working solution? (This helps create a working product right away.)

○ Can you collaborate with a customer whose business can generate enough revenue to support your company? (This insures that your company can survive and generate a profit from day one.)

	Old Rules	New Rules
Creating an Idea	❏ Look for a unique idea that nobody else has though of.	❏ Look for a Holy Grail problem that everyone has already thought about.
Solving a Problem	❏ Create a product that solves any problem.	❏ Create a product that solves a Holy Grail problem.
Creating a Product	❏ Create a product and then market it. The focus is on having a uniqe idea for a product.	❏ Collaborate with customers to create a product and a market at the same time. The focus is on using existing technology (the not-so Holy Grail) to solve a Holy Grail type problem.
Long-Term Goal	❏ Become the dominant leader in the market.	❏ Create a product, in collaboration with a customer, that the customer has helped design and create. This closely ties the customer to your company.
		❏ Sell the product to other customers who have similar problems. Use existing customers to generate revenue and apply the reputation of existing customers to make it easier to attract new customers.

Table 5-1. Comparison of Old and New Rules of Creating an Idea for a Product

○ Can you collaborate with a customer who can help you market your product to others? (This can lower your cost for marketing and selling to others.)

○ Can you collaborate with a customer who might be attractive to a potential suitor? (This increases the chance that your company may be acquired.)

Remember, an idea is only as good as the way you apply it.

6

Designing a Company to be Acquired

Nine out of ten startups fail. Surviving long enough to issue stock through an IPO is still no guarantee of success. Wall Street is littered with the remnants of once powerful companies (Pets.com, WebVan, and Ricochet, a wireless Internet service that had once hired Al Gore as its spokesman) that went through a successful IPO, but ultimately crashed and burned. If your only path to success and profitability rests on your hope of a successful IPO and subsequent growth, the odds are heavily against you. That doesn't mean you shouldn't try to become the next Google success story, but it does mean that pinning your future on a long shot is no better than pinning your entire retirement on buying a winning lottery ticket.

That's why I advocate that you create a startup as an attractive acquisition target from its inception. This still leaves open the possibility of hitting it big as an IPO, but it also leaves open the possibility of growing into a larger company or being acquired by another company.

Companies not designed from the start to be acquired have no choice but to succeed on their own. When the online grocery store WebVan, began, they pursued the single-minded strategy of going for an IPO. Then they promptly burned through billions of dollars of investors' money, leaving them with little choice. They either had to go for broke and earn back all those billions, or go bankrupt. Saddled with such huge debts, they went bankrupt.

Consider how different this story might have been if WebVan had designed themselves as an acquisition target from the start. Because WebVan saw the established supermarkets as direct competitors, they spent billions creating their own infrastructure, essentially duplicating the infrastructure of warehouses and delivery trucks that the brick and mortar supermarkets had taken decades to establish and refine.

The main idea behind WebVan was online shopping and home delivery of your groceries, so they could have focused on their core competency and made alliances with the established supermarkets. In exchange for using the supermarkets' existing infrastructure, WebVan could have bought their products from these supermarkets and given them an additional source of revenue.

Since none of the existing supermarkets were offering online grocery shopping and home delivery at that time, this could have given WebVan a fast and far less expensive route to profitability. By not duplicating the traditional supermarket infrastructure, WebVan would have been perfectly positioned as an acquisition target. Any supermarket that bought out WebVan could have added a new service.

Once WebVan sunk billions into duplicating a supermarket's infrastructure, it immediately eliminated any possibility of being acquired. Few supermarkets would want the added cost of a duplicate infrastructure to support and maintain. By not designing WebVan as an acquisition target, its founders gave the company only one chance to succeed and that was through the long shot of an IPO and subsequent growth. Because the odds were stacked against them, it's no surprise that WebVan failed a few billion dollars later.

In retrospect, consider these three possible outcomes that WebVan could have chosen to pursue:

○ Spend billions creating an infrastructure for future growth and hope that revenue can increase fast enough to cover these massive costs. This is the option they chose, which led to failure.

○ Establish the company as an acquisition target, make strategic alliances with companies that already had the necessary infrastructure in place, and grow organically. This would have still allowed the company to build its own infrastructure later if they wished, by using existing profits to pay for it. This would have led to slower growth, but would have enabled long-term survival.

○ Establish the company as an acquisition target in order to sell out to a larger company that would find WebVan's infrastructure a complement, not a duplicate, of its own infrastructure, thus allowing WebVan to be smoothly integrated into the acquiring company.

While every entrepreneur may dream about creating a company that becomes the next dominant leader in its field, the reality is that you must plan from day one to succeed at all stages of your company's growth. You limit your chance of becoming a leader by ignoring the greater chance that you can still make money while never growing beyond a small company.

Given a choice between failure and bankruptcy or success and profitability, it's in your best interests to do everything in your power to insure your company's profitability no matter what happens. You can never control outside circumstances and random chance, but you can control your company's ability to make money by strategically designing it to both grow big and to be an attractive acquisition target at the same time.

UNDERSTANDING ATTRACTIVE ACQUISITION TARGETS

To design your company as an acquisition target, you must understand why companies acquire other companies. The more you can design your company to match common reasons for acquiring another company, the more attractive your company will be. Some reasons a company might make an acquisition include:

○ To expand its product line quickly

○ To expand into new markets quickly

○ To acquire the technology or personnel in another company

○ To eliminate a competitor

○ To expand market share with duplicate products

Acquiring Another Company's Products

One of the more common reasons for an acquisition is to gain control over another company's products or services. While a large corporation could spend the time and resources developing a similar product, it's usually not practical. First, creating a new product takes time and requires extra resources. Second, and more importantly, marketing a similar product, even if it's superior to an existing one, is an uphill battle that requires more resources to compete against a rival product that's already entrenched in the market. Even then, the chances of taking away market share from an established rival will likely be a long and drawn out process.

Simply buying another company and taking control of that other company's products represents a fast way for any corporation to expand its product line with best-of-breed products that have already been established as leaders in their field.

At one time, Symantec was a general-purpose software publisher that sold outlining software, presentation software, and language compilers for both PC and Macintosh computers. One problem with this product line was that it competed directly against Microsoft's own growing product line. Symantec had a choice. It could continue to compete against Microsoft (and probably lose), or it could expand into other markets that would insure long-term survival and profitability for the company.

Symantec wisely chose this later option and acquired a small company called Peter Norton Computing, which specialized in selling software utilities and diagnostic programs for repairing hard disks or retrieving deleted files.

By expanding into this new market of software utilities, Symantec gained a new source of profits. This eventually helped to save the company when its mainstream applications and language compilers ran into tougher competition. Eventually Symantec dumped all of its mainstream products and focused entirely on their growing software utilities market.

The company soon expanded from software diagnostics to computer security, which led to the introduction of antivirus software, firewalls, and intrusion detection software for both the consumer market and the much more profitable enterprise market. If Symantec had tried to create its own software utilities and diagnostic programs from scratch, they might not have succeeded. By acquiring another company, Symantec could grow quickly and ultimately became one of the leaders in the field of computer security and software utilities.

Expanding Into New Markets

A second reason why corporations acquire other companies is to expand into new markets. A smaller company may have found a niche that the larger corporation isn't competing in. Once this smaller company grows and remains profitable, it becomes an attractive acquisition target. Essentially a larger corporation can buy out the smaller company to get profitability and market share in a new area overnight.

This was actually the strategy that Microsoft used to dominant the operating system market. Initially Microsoft focused on creating compilers for creating programs using the BASIC programming language. Microsoft's entire business model revolved around providing a BASIC compiler for different personal computers.

When Microsoft found out that IBM was shopping for an operating system for their IBM personal computer, Bill Gates started looking for a company that sold an operating system so that they could expand into the operating system market. They found a one-man company run by a programmer named Tim Paterson, who had created a simple operating system called QDOS (Quick and Dirty Operating System).

Microsoft bought the rights to QDOS, renamed it PC-DOS for IBM, and renamed it a second time as MS-DOS for other personal computers that were similar and compatible with the original IBM PC. By buying out a tiny company, Microsoft expanded into a new market and eventually became the dominant leader in the operating system market.

If it had never acquired another company, Microsoft might have forever remained a niche company providing BASIC compilers for the personal computer market. By taking advantage of a new opportunity, Microsoft's acquisition helped the company grow far beyond its original goals.

Acquiring the Resources of Another Company

Sometimes another company's products aren't as attractive as the people or technology behind the company itself. Back in the '90s, Apple had their own engineers involved in designing the microprocessor chips used in their products, including the Macintosh computer and their personal digital assistant dubbed the Newton. By using their own engineers, Apple could optimize microprocessors for their products in a way they could not if they used off-the-shelf parts.

To save money and lower costs, Apple eventually decided to switch to microprocessors made by Intel, the largest chip manufacturer in the world. By taking advantage of Intel's massive resources and economies of scale, Apple hoped to use Intel's processors in all of their products to lower their own costs.

However, Apple's executives soon realized that getting rid of their microprocessor engineers also made them more dependent on Intel while making it harder to optimize or custom design processors for their own products. Although Apple's iPhone has proved to be a big hit, Apple reportedly had to make compromises in the iPhone's microprocessors. These microprocessors weren't what Apple really wanted or needed, but they managed to make the best of it anyway.

At this point, the people at Apple decided they wanted their own capability to design microprocessors to customize them for their own products, which was something they couldn't do by relying on outside vendors like Intel. Rather than hire new microprocessor engineers and spend time and money creating their own microprocessor engineering division, Apple chose the faster route of acquiring another company, called PA Semi, instead.

PA Semi sold microprocessors commonly used outside of the personal computer market. One of PA Semi's biggest customers was the Department of Defense. When Apple acquired PA Semi, they didn't do it to expand into the defense contracting business or the microprocessor design business. Apple acquired PA Semi solely for the engineers and technical expertise of the company.

Armed with PA Semi's technical knowledge, Apple can now customize its own microprocessors again and optimize them for its own products including the iPhone. Instead of being at the mercy of outside microprocessor vendors like Intel, Apple can rely on itself. Instead of selling products like the iPhone that contain parts that any competitor could purchase and duplicate, Apple can now create its own processors that nobody else can duplicate or even buy without Apple's approval.

PA Semi won't help Apple break into new markets, but it will help Apple maintain its technological edge against rivals for its existing markets, and that alone might make the acquisition of PA Semi pay off in the long run.

Eliminating a Competitor

One common quip about the oil industry is that if an inventor ever created an engine that could run off water, the oil companies would buy up the rights so that the invention (or the inventor) would never be seen or heard from again. This story points out another reason corporations acquire smaller companies. If it's not practical to compete, then it's often less expensive just to buy out the competition instead.

For years, Adobe (publishers of the popular Photoshop software for editing digital images) fought with their main rival, Macromedia. While Adobe's Photoshop had the digital editing field locked up, Macromedia had established two products that dominated their own field: Dreamweaver (a web page designing program) and Flash (a web page animation design program). Every professional web page designer used Dreamweaver and Flash along with Photoshop.

Initially Adobe tried to compete against Macromedia with two rival products called GoLive and LiveMotion. GoLive was Adobe's web page designing program meant to knock off Dreamweaver. LiveMotion was Adobe's animation program meant to take out Flash. After spending several years developing GoLive and LiveMotion and marketing them as compatible and integrated with Photoshop, Adobe wound up spending millions without much success. Dreamweaver remained as popular as ever and every web page designer kept using Flash.

Adobe could have kept fighting, but the company realized that it was spending money on a near hopeless cause, so it decided to acquire Macromedia instead. After buying Macromedia, Adobe quickly dumped GoLive and LiveMotion and now market Macromedia's products under their own name as Adobe Dreamweaver and Adobe Flash.

Just by acquiring their rival, Adobe immediately gained possession of the dominant market share for web page designing software, which the engineers had failed to establish on their own. Adobe could have saved money if it had just decided to acquire Macromedia from the start instead of wasting time and money trying to develop rival programs that the market rejected.

More importantly, now that Adobe has ownership of three dominant leaders (Photoshop, Dreamweaver, and Flash), it has a nearly impregnable position in the market that no other rivals can possibly compete against. By eliminating their chief competitor in the graphics and web page industry, Adobe now represents the only dominant products to choose from.

Expanding market share with duplicate products

Rather than eliminating a rival, it can be more profitable to allow that rival to thrive—just as long as the profits from that rival product flow back to your own company. That's the theory behind Hewlett-Packard's acquisition of Compaq Computers.

Both Hewlett-Packard and Compaq Computers sold personal computers to consumers and enterprise customers. With most acquisitions, one company's products get promoted while the other company's products get discontinued. However, customers had developed relationships and loyalty to both Hewlett-Packard and Compaq computers. Technically, the internal components might be similar (or even identical), but eliminating one brand name over the other risked losing market share. So Hewlett-Packard decided to keep both brands.

Compaq might still seem like a competitor to Hewlett-Packard, but whether you buy a Hewlett-Packard computer or a Compaq computer, the profits are still flowing to a single company. Trying to dominate an industry with one brand name can be difficult. If you can add two or more brand names, each individual brand name might not dominate, but collectively they'll hold more market share than they could by themselves. In the case of Hewlett-Packard, acquiring Compaq Computers helped them expand their market share faster than they could possibly do by promoting the single brand of Hewlett-Packard alone.

UNDERSTANDING UNATTRACTIVE ACQUISITION TARGETS

Once you understand some of the reasons why corporations want to acquire smaller companies, you should also understand what makes certain companies unattractive as potential acquisitions. First, and most importantly, is cost. Every company can be worth acquiring at the right price, but no company is worth acquiring at the wrong price. If a company's price seems too high, a potential suitor will decide the price isn't worth it and look elsewhere.

A more serious problem with acquiring companies can be hidden liabilities. Perhaps the target company really isn't as profitable as it might seem, hiding huge amounts of debt through creative bookkeeping. Maybe the target company is fighting a lawsuit that it could lose, making a potential acquiring company liable for any monetary damages.

A company interested in making an acquisition must examine all contracts and legal agreements the acquisition target has made with its customers and suppliers. Some legal arrangements can make a company less attractive, such as agreeing to sell its products far below cost to a customer for a fixed number of years, or agreeing to provide another company (which could be a rival to a potential acquiring company) with valuable technology.

Even worse, a target company may be attractive only for a limited time frame. If market conditions change too rapidly, that target company may no longer be worth acquiring.

Mattel made this mistake back in 1999 when it paid $3.5 billion to acquire The Learning Company, a publisher of educational software for children with popular products such as Reader Rabbit, Myst, Carmen Sandiego, and National Geographic. Mattel believed that it could expand its toy business to include computer software.

Unfortunately for Mattel, it soon discovered that the educational software market never grew as fast as predicted. Unlike business applications that generated revenue through upgrades, educational software rarely needed upgrades. A program that taught multiplication to children would work today and ten years later without needing any changes.

Instead of earning $50 million as Mattel had projected, The Learning Company wound up losing $105 million. By 2000, Mattel was losing $1.5 million a day with The Learning Company. Mattel eventually sold The Learning Company to Gores Technology for nothing more than a percentage of The Learning Company's future profits, essentially writing off its entire $3.5 billion initial investment as a complete loss.

The problem wasn't that The Learning Company didn't produce decent products, but that the window of opportunity for educational software had passed. Buy a great company at the wrong time and you'll still wind up losing, just as if you had bought the wrong company in the first place.

MAKING YOUR COMPANY AN ATTRACTIVE ACQUISITION TARGET

By understanding what makes a good acquisition target and what makes a poor one, you'll have a better idea about how to steer your own startup to make it attractive to another company:

○ Target a niche market

○ Target a new market

○ Develop superior technology and attract the best talent

Look for a niche market. A niche market can still be profitable; it just may not be massively profitable. While the market for accounting software is very large, there's also a great deal of competition. However, there's far less competition in a niche market, such as one that uses accounting software for medical billing. By targeting a niche market, your company's products can complement a larger corporation's product line, making your company an attractive acquisition target.

Another approach is to target a new market where there is no established leader. Such new markets don't last long until an established leader emerges, but by gaining a stake in a new market, your company can be attractive to another company that wants to jump into that same market as quickly as possible.

When spyware programs first popped up on computers, bombarding users with pop-up ads, the market for anti-spyware programs was wide open. Large, established companies tend to react slowly, which gave several anti-spyware companies the opportunity to carve out their stake in the market. Now that the anti-spyware market has matured, many of these anti-spyware companies are primed to be acquired by the larger security companies that didn't move into this new market fast enough.

Your company should produce high-quality products and service, but the more you can establish your company's reputation as superior to competitors, the more attractive your company will be to those looking to buy instant brand name recognition. Back in 1992, Christopher Klaus developed one of the first programs to scan another computer for flaws and loopholes that a hacker could exploit. This initial program, dubbed Internet Scanner, soon became recognized as one of the leading security scanning tools. Christopher then founded a company, Internet Security Systems (ISS), to market the product in 1994. By 1998, ISS had gone public through an IPO and the company soon developed a suite of additional computer security programs.

Not wanting to get left out of the suddenly growing computer security market, IBM decided to purchase the technology and the brand name recognition of ISS for $1.3 billion in 2006. Having the technical reputation of ISS, plus having the added benefit of the brains behind this technology, turned IBM overnight into an established leader in the computer security market.

When you start up your own company, first identify several possible companies that you respect that could acquire your company. Next, follow the announcements in business publications, such as the *Wall Street Journal, Red Herring,* and *Business Week,* to track which companies have been acquired in the past and the reasons why.

As a game, try to guess which companies a larger corporation might acquire next based on their product lines and their goals. Now picture your own company's product line and find a way to mold your company to fit into a potential suitor's needs.

By designing your company to be acquired, you have the dual option of growing or being acquired. Your company still has the chance to become that one in ten that survives long enough to go public through an IPO to become a profitable and dominant leader in its industry. But if your company falls in with those nine out of ten that never survive long enough to go public, you'll still have a way to make money.

When a larger company acquires a smaller, profitable company, the potential payoff can be worth several millions or even a billion. This makes it nearly equal to the payoff from going public, except with a nine times greater chance of success. Setting up your company to be acquired is nothing more than setting your company up for success in whatever form that requires, and that should be the goal of every entrepreneur no matter what business you're in.

	Old Rules	New Rules
Business Model	❐ Compete against established leaders.	❐ Cooperate with established leaders.
Market Focus	❐ Enter an established market.	❐ Create a new market or target a niche market.
Human Resources	❐ Hire the best people to create a superior product.	❐ Hire the best people to create a superior product and use those employees to make your company an attractive acquisition target.
Long-Term Goal	❐ Become big enough to acquire other companies.	❐ Become valuable enough to attract an acquiring company.

Table 6-1. Comparison of Old and New Rules of Designing a Company

7

Collaborating with the Customer

Every business has a customer. Whether you're a one-person vendor selling hot dogs on the street or a multinational corporation with factories and offices on three separate continents, your business depends on your customers. The sole focus of every business is to sell a product or service to a customer to make a profit.

Perhaps the most important factor in any company's success lies in choosing customers who ultimately define your path to success. A hot dog vendor on the street may seem helpless about choosing his customers, but the truth is that even a hot dog vendor has a choice of customers.

Place a hot dog cart near Wall Street and you'll wind up catering to people in the financial sector. Place that same hot dog cart near the beach and you'll wind up selling more hot dogs to tourists and families. One key to choosing your customers is location. Find the type of customers you want to cater to and then go to that location where you'll find those types of customers.

Many businesses fail for two reasons. First, they don't know who their best customers may be. The best customer isn't always the one that spends the most, but the one who generates the greatest long-term revenue. Second, businesses don't always actively look for their best customers. Instead, too many businesses rely on chance and luck and hope that their best customers will find them.

Every product can be sold as long as you find the right types of customers who want to buy it. The "build it and they will come" mentality may work in movies, but it rarely works in real life. If you focus on building a superior product, you still need to identify your best customers. If you build a mediocre product but find exactly who your best customers are and where you can find them, you can make a small fortune.

Remember, the quality of any product doesn't determine the success of a business. Finding your best customers determines the success of your business. The more focused you are on how wonderful or unique your idea for a product may be, the more likely you'll overlook the crucial step of finding your best customers.

The secret to finding your best customers? Collaborate with them and let them tell you what they really want.

TYPES OF CUSTOMERS

In general, there are two types of customers: individuals and businesses. A hot dog vendor typically caters to individuals while many corporations cater solely to other businesses, such as a company that provides payroll and billing services to other companies. Of course, some businesses cater to both individuals and corporations, such as Federal Express or Citibank.

As an entrepreneur, start by identifying which type of customers your product should target. Sometimes the less obvious choice may wind up being more lucrative. For example, if you're a chef, the obvious choice might be opening a restaurant and selling meals directly to individuals. A less obvious, and potentially more lucrative choice, might be preparing meals and selling them to the airline industry.

While you can make a fortune selling to individuals (think of Starbucks, McDonald's, or Wal-Mart), it's often more lucrative to sell to corporations. Spend time closing a sale to an individual and you might sell one item. Spend the same amount of time closing a sale to a corporation and you might sell hundreds or even thousands of items. Dell Computers sells computers to individuals and corporations, but can you guess which side of their business brings in greater revenue per sale?

Whether you sell to individuals or corporations, the most expensive part of running any business is finding new customers. The cost for getting a new customer, through advertising, sales, and marketing, is many times greater than selling to an existing customer who already knows and trusts your business. So the ideal product is one that you can sell to the same customer over and over again.

Supermarkets operate on razor thin profit margins, yet they can repeatedly sell to the same customers because everyone has to eat. Customers may need the services of an asphalt paving company, but not nearly as frequently as they need to buy groceries. Supermarkets can rely on repeat customers while an asphalt paving company cannot. That's why supermarkets (or companies like Starbucks and Wal-Mart) can rely on individuals while asphalt paving companies often rely on businesses (paving over parking lots) and individuals (paving driveways).

Sales are simply a function of time and revenue. The most lucrative markets are either selling to individuals as repeat customers, or selling to corporations, as shown in Figure 7-1. If you can sell a product or service on a regular basis to corporations, you can possibly achieve the highest profits of all, which is what makes companies like IBM so powerful and profitable.

The time and expense needed to attract a new customer means that catering to individuals is only profitable if you have a line of products that you can sell to that same customer. If you only have one product that an individual will buy, you'll need to find a new customer each time (expensive), make a huge profit on each sale (to justify the expense of finding new customers constantly), or find a way to sell additional products to that same customer. A vacuum cleaner company might have a huge profit

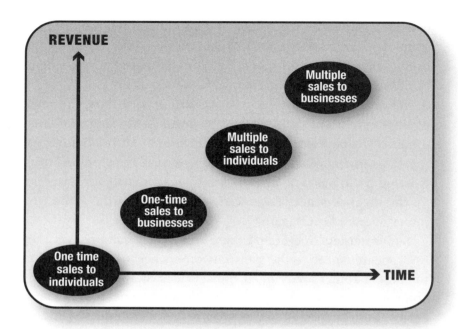

Figure 7-1. Comparing Revenue vs. Time

margin on each vacuum cleaner or might sell additional acces-
sories that the customer may buy with the vacuum cleaner or
sometime in the future.

To repeatedly sell to the same customers, you need either
multiple products or a consumable product such as food, vita-
mins, toothpaste, or shampoo; anything that gets used up and
needs to be replaced. You can think of a service as a consumable
product. A payroll and billing service is something that companies not only need, but need regularly.

Your product and your creativity define the type of customer
your business may reach. One reason that software is so lucrative a product is that the expense of duplicating and distributing
it is next to nothing. Any hobbyist programmer can spend a
weekend creating a useful program and make duplicate copies of
that program at no extra cost. Distributing that program is

equally simple over the Internet, giving a one-man programmer company a global reach without any added expense.

High-technology products, such as computer programs, cost virtually nothing to create and distribute. If you can make multiple sales of your product to repeat customers (including corporations), your costs will be low and your profit margins high. That's the basic formula for companies like Microsoft.

TALKING TO YOUR CUSTOMERS

As an entrepreneur, you probably have a great idea for a product. This is the point where many entrepreneurs think they know who their customers might be and what they need. So they'll rush to create a product and deliver it to the market—only to find out that their product doesn't really do what customers need or that the people who they thought would be their best customers really don't need or want the product. Now, the entrepreneur must spend additional time and money redesigning the product and determining who really might need the product, which he (or she) should have done in the first place.

Designing a product without identifying either your potential customers or the most pressing needs of your customers is like trying to tailor a suit of clothes for someone you've never seen. Chances are whatever you design won't quite fit and you'll need to redesign the whole thing anyway.

Since you have the power to design your product, you also have the power to choose the type of customers you want by the way you design (and market) your product. If your product falls under the category of a one-time sale to an individual, you must either raise your profit margin per sale or lower your cost of duplicating and distributing your product (such as a computer program).

Raise the price of your product to give a high profit margin, and your natural market is now a high-end consumer. Most people aren't going to buy a Lamborghini two or three times a month, so the company must price their car in the six-figures to earn a profit on each individual sale. Knowing this, the company would be foolish to target middle class or lower-class families. Instead, Lamborghini only targets the wealthy consumer market.

In targeting the likely class of customers for your product, identify who might need your product. The need doesn't necessarily have to be crucial. Everyone needs food, but not everyone wants to eat at Taco Bell. Billionaires might need a car, but what they also need is a car that reflects their status and satisfies their ego. In that sense, an ordinary car from Ford won't meet that need, while a Lamborghini would.

Before you spend time and money building your product, the most important step you can take is identifying your customers first. The simplest way to identify your customers is to find who you think they might be. Then ask them what they want.

If the people you thought would be your best customers don't want your product, you must either find customers who do want your product, or you must change your product. In either case, talking to potential customers first can keep you from wasting time and money creating and marketing a product that nobody needs.

Typically, entrepreneurs target a certain market and identify their customers generically as the "medical community" or "financial institutions." To succeed, you need to go beyond such vague descriptions and pinpoint actual companies who might be your customers. Perhaps the best way to validate who your customers may be is through collaboration.

Collaborating essentially means contacting companies within your target market (such as "financial institutions") and talking to the people within that corporation. The goal at this early stage isn't to sell your product to anyone, but to find out:

○ Do potential customers in your target market even need your product?

○ What is really the biggest problem that your product needs to solve?

If you don't involve your potential customers early in your startup's product design, you may be surprised how far off the mark you may be. Companies may start off creating one product and then discover that their entire business model is designed for a market that doesn't exist.

Back in 1981 a company called Context Management Systems created and marketed the first integrated software application for personal computers, dubbed Context MBA. Since it was the first company to offer integrated software that included a word processor, spreadsheet, database, and charting program, it had tremendous first-mover advantage. Unfortunately, the company focused their entire business model on selling the program to run on different types of personal computers.

While dozens of different personal computers existed back in 1981, the market soon settled on a single standard: the IBM PC. As a result, the market no longer needed a program capable of running on different types of personal computers, essentially taking away Context MBA's greatest advantage.

Since computers back then had limited processing power, another problem emerged. The program crammed in too many features that required too many system resources, causing the software to run extremely slowly, to the point of being nearly unusable.

Context MBA offered the market a multi-platform program loaded with multiple features. However, what the market really wanted was a program that ran on the IBM PC and offered a handful of features that ran quickly. The market ignored Context MBA and chose a much smaller, product with fewer features called Lotus 1-2-3.

What killed Context MBA were its technical issues. The company poured all its resources designing a product for a nonexistent market. However, businesses can also fail when they ignore situations that only potential customers would know about. For example, the best ideas for products are often transplanted from one field and applied to another. Unfortunately, transplanting a familiar idea to a new field isn't always a guarantee of success.

Browse the Internet and you can find dozens of web sites that offers price comparisons of different items, such as digital cameras and laptop computers. Just type in the product you want and these web sites list the available prices for the exact same item. Now you can buy the product you want at the lowest possible price.

Applying this same idea, one entrepreneur came up with a business to identify the best prices and subscription plans for cellular phones. The idea was simple. Just type in your zip code and this web site would identify the best coverage in your area and the prices for phones and subscription plans from different mobile phone carriers.

Here's why this startup might have failed. First, the entrepreneur didn't do his homework and created a product without consulting with potential customers to find out what they really wanted. As it turns out, being able to find the best coverage and lowest prices was nice, but it was more of a luxury compared to another factor. Often people don't choose a mobile phone carrier based on coverage (which they don't know), but on what mobile phone carrier their friends or family are using so they can take advantage of incentive plans that allow free calling between family members on the same network.

A second reason why this startup might have failed was that it relied on the cooperation of the various cellular companies to provide up to date pricing along with their coverage information. What happened was that these cellular phone companies didn't want to reveal their coverage (or lack of coverage) in certain areas, since this might drive customers to rivals.

Cellular phone companies especially didn't want to reveal their different pricing plans when they often had a variety of pricing plans to meet a customer's needs. The last thing cellular companies wanted was for customers to choose a lower pricing plan (if they knew it existed).

In this case, the entrepreneur failed to identify two customers: the individual consumer, who would visit the web site, and the cellular phone companies, who could benefit from having potential customers directed to their subscription plans.

Because this startup didn't meet the customer's needs, and it didn't get the cooperation from the companies it needed to make the service accurate and worthwhile, this business idea ultimately failed.

Besides failing to meet the needs of real customers, this startup also failed to solve a pressing problem. For individuals, the pressing problem wasn't to find the best coverage or necessarily the lowest subscription plans, but to find the most convenient cellular network to use. As far as the goals of the cellular phone companies, their goal wasn't to share information about their coverage plans in order to compete with others over the best coverage and lowest price, but simply to attract customers to their most profitable subscription plans.

Consider how this situation could have turned out if the entrepreneur had collaborated with his potential customers to discover that individuals didn't really want or need this service, and that cellular companies didn't want to cooperate in sharing coverage and pricing plan information. The entrepreneur could have killed this idea and pursued another one, saving him time and money in the process. Or he might have modified his idea to meet the real needs of his customers.

Perhaps he could have made the cellular phone companies his real customers and designed his product to solve the cellular phone company's urgent problem of gaining more subscribers and keeping existing subscribers from defecting to rival serv-

Astrophysicist Chuck Bower created a unique computer program. Instead of calculating particles flying around in space, Chuck created a computer program that analyzes situations in football games and calculates the plays with the best odds of success. The idea is for coaches to run the program to help them decide what to do next. According to Chuck, the program works, but nobody wants to try it.

While costly (the program runs in the six figures), the real problem is that Chuck can't get anyone to try his program. Despite meeting with a handful of teams, including the New England Patriots and the Indianapolis Colts, no coach has felt the need to rely on a computer program to make their decisions for them.

The program, named Zeus, analyzes decisions by simulating a potential outcome multiple times until it finds a play that offers the greatest chance of victory. According to its creator, most teams make enough wrong decisions to ultimately cost them one or two victories a season.

Part of the problem is that the NFL doesn't allow

ices. A sales person for a cellular company might want to type in a zip code to receive information about new businesses in that area that might need a business cellular subscription plan for its employees.

One of the biggest reasons companies fail is because they either target the wrong customers or create a product that potential customers don't need. Talk to you potential customers. Your business depends on it.

COLLABORATION CREATES A LOYAL CUSTOMER

Come up with a great idea and within a few months someone will come up with a copycat idea to steal customers away from you. That's why a great idea by itself is never enough to run a company. You need both a good idea and strategic implementation of that idea at the same time.

What you need to do is approach a potential customer, identify their most pressing problem that needs to be solved, and then design a product to solve that customer's problem.

Since you won't fully understand the problem, you'll need the customer to tell you. Since the customers can't solve the problem themselves, they'll need you to build it for them. Such a close collaboration allows you to create the exact product that the customer needs.

Now if conditions change and the customer needs new features or changes to the existing ones, they have two choices: switch to a rival product or continue collaborating with you to redesign a new product. Switching to a rival product is never an easy decision, but it's far less likely if the customer themselves had a stake in designing your product. Close collaboration with the customer insures that the customer gets the product that he or she needs and has a compelling reason to stay with your product and your company.

While you may never have heard of the Immersion Corporation, you may have used their product that is embedded inside the latest mobile telephones, video game consoles, or automotive controls. Immersion specializes in tactile feedback technology, embedded in other company's

computers on the sidelines, so a program like Zeus couldn't be used anyway. A more important reason is that Zeus is the type of program that coaches don't really want. Allowing a computer program to make decisions takes away the excitement of coaching and making decisions yourself. No matter how great this Zeus play-predicting program may be, its failure stems less from its technical capabilities and more from its failure to address the needs of its actual customers—the coaches who must rely on its predictions.

Zeus is a classic example of a product in search of a market. Since the market is so small (NFL teams) and the customers in that market have already rejected it, the chances for success is likely to be close to nothing. Zeus proves that even a great idea will never work if your only potential customers don't want it. For this entrepreneur, a better solution would be asking coaches what they really want and then building a product that meets those needs.

products, such as smartphones with touchscreens. When you press a button displayed on a touchscreen, the smartphone may vibrate slightly to give you tactile feedback that you pressed the button correctly.

Once another company has Immersion's tactile feedback technology embedded in its products, switching to a competitor's products will be much more troublesome. It's easier just to continue using Immersion's technology. Immersion had to collaborate its various customers to get its technology to work in other companies' products, but now that Immersion is as an integral feature of that product, Immersion holds a dominant position with each of their customers.

CHOOSE A STRATEGIC CUSTOMER FOR COLLABORATION

When you collaborate with a customer in order to design a product, you want a solution tailor-made for the customer. You can also sell it to other customers who need similar solutions. That's why choosing a customer to collaborate with can be so crucial. Collaborate with the wrong customer and you may wind up with a solution that only that particular customer can use. Collaborate with a strategic customer and you can create a solution that others can use and are willing to buy too.

A strategic customer is one that is both representative of your target customer and possesses a reputation as a leader in its field. For example, if your company sells medical billing software, you could customize and sell your product to any hospital in the country, or you could focus on a hospital with a reputation for using cutting-edge technology or that specializes in certain types of research.

Your product's close association with a well-known and reputable customer validates your product in the market place in the same way that celebrity endorsements validate soft drinks or running shoes in the eyes of the public. Gain a strategic customer as a collaborator and you define the right product to solve a pressing need to generate revenue from day one, and you leverage the reputation of the strategic customer to help sell your product to similar customers.

Ironically, one of Google's initial customers was Yahoo!. Yahoo! contracted with Google to provide the underlying search technology for their web portal. Initially Yahoo! had the reputation of being the most popular search engine on the Internet. By working with Yahoo!, Google gained a strategic customer that provided revenue and gave Google credibility as a search engine.

Perhaps the final, and most important, purpose of a strategic customer is to help your company to get acquired. Once you collaborate with a strategic customer, you develop a relationship with that customer who has helped to shape the design of your product. A fast way for a larger corporation to gain your strategic customer as their own customer is to buy out your company. By buying out your company, a larger corporation essentially buys the assets and customer base that your company has created.

The more important your strategic customers are to others and the closer these strategic customers are linked to your own company (through their involvement in designing your product), the more attractive your company becomes as an acquisition target.

Any corporation that buys out your company will inherit your customers. Sometimes during an acquisition, customers may leave a company that's being acquired if their business relationship changes. However, if you've collaborated with your customers and linked them closely to your startup, customers will be far less likely to switch to a rival product. This helps to guarantee that the majority of your customer base will remain intact for the acquiring company.

COLLABORATION BEGINS BEFORE
THE DESIGN PHASE

The common belief among entrepreneurs is that you need to build a killer product to have customers naturally flock to your door. The hard truth is that having a great product is never enough. The truth is that collaboration is far more important since it keeps you from building the wrong product or trying to market the right product to the wrong customers.

First, identify a Holy Grail problem that represents a pressing need that must be solved. Next, design a not-so Holy Grail solution with the collaboration of a strategic customer. This strategic customer isn't necessarily the one that will generate the biggest profit, but the one who will enhance your company's reputation and customer base in the eyes of a potential suitor who might want to acquire your company.

Finally, give a company a reason to acquire your own startup by closely tying a strategic customer to your own company. This gives potential suitors a choice of either creating a duplicate solution to compete directly against you (time-consuming) or just acquiring your company instead, giving you maximum pay-out in the minimal amount of time.

Ultimately, your company's success is directly linked to your collaboration with your customers. Customer collaboration creates the following benefits:

○ Your customers help you design the right product for their most pressing problems right now.

○ Your customers help generate revenue for your company from day one.

○ Your customers can give your company credibility.

○ Your customers help make your company more valuable in the eyes of a potential acquirer.

	Old Rules	New Rules
Customer Focus	❐ Sell to everyone (corporations and individuals).	❐ Only sell to strategic customers. (corporations).
Business Model	❐ Build a product and convince customers to buy it.	❐ Collaborate with customers to build the exact product they need.
Dealing with Competition	❐ Get the first-mover advantage.	❐ Collaborate with customers to make their ideas part of the product so they have a strong reason to avoid competing products.
Long-Term Goal	❐ Constantly increase market share.	❐ Grab enough strategic customers to make the company's customer base attractive to a potential acquirer.

Table 7-1. Comparison of Old and New Rules for Dealing with Customers

8

Case Studies of Failures

Starting up a company isn't easy. It takes a lot of work and money just to create a company, and changing market conditions can kill a startup overnight. Think of all those startups relying on proprietary communication systems that wound up getting wiped out when the Internet took over.

While luck plays a huge role in a company's success or failure, too often a company's failure can be attributed to mistakes that could have been easily avoided with a little foresight. Sometimes a company succeeds not necessarily because the entrepreneur had a wonderful idea in a perfect market, but because the entrepreneur simply avoided some pitfalls.

A company can fail in many ways, at any time, during any phase. Although companies can be their most vulnerable during the startup phase, they can also fail in the growth or scaling phase. Just because a company starts earning a profit doesn't mean that it can't suddenly fail three months later. Running a company is a constant, ongoing activity. Neglect one part of your business and you could bring your entire company crashing down around you.

By studying different types of failures, you can avoid the same traps that tripped up so many promising startups. Often the difference between failure and success can be as simple as a single decision.

STARTUP PHASE FAILURES

The start-up phase is when an entrepreneur puts a company together. This can be the most crucial time for any startup since this is where you lay the foundation for the company by defining its product, target market, and strategy. If you fail to design your startup correctly from its inception, you could be aiming your company in the wrong direction and wind up missing crucial markets as a result. For many startups, these early mistakes are costly enough to keep a company from ever becoming profitable, even if it has the best product in the world.

The Trap of Product-Focused Thinking

Don't focus on your product. Focus on how your product can meet the needs of a customer. Too many times entrepreneurs fall in love with their product and design it in a vacuum, creating a product that they think people will want. The end result is that the entrepreneur winds up creating a product that's close to what people want, but not necessarily close enough to make many people want to buy it. When this happens, the entrepreneur must go back and redesign the product to meet the customer's needs, wasting time and money in the process.

To avoid this problem, always collaborate with the customer early in the design process. You may find that all the features you thought were necessary can be dropped (saving time and money), or you may find that your product is missing major features altogether.

PointCast Network is a classic example of focusing on the product and not on the customer. Back in 1996, PointCast created a screensaver that displayed news and other information delivered live over the Internet. The PointCast Network used push technology, which was a hot concept at the time, and received enormous press coverage.

Unfortunately, the product did not perform as well as expected, partly because it gobbled up bandwidth. Corporations banned its use and most individuals at that time connected to the Internet through dial-up connections that couldn't handle the program's bandwidth requirements. Even worse, people objected to the large number of advertisements that appeared along with the news.

In 1997 News Corporation offered to purchase the company for $450 million, but PointCast turned this offer down. Two years later in 1999, when the company's product proved a failure, PointCast sold themselves for only $7 million.

PointCast highlights two problems. First, if you don't talk to your customers to ask what they need, you'll likely create a product that most people won't want. Nobody knows the problems to solve better than your potential customers, so the sooner you get them involved in the design process, the sooner you'll create the right product to sell to your customers.

Second, if you try to grow your company and fail, your company's value can plummet like a rock. In PointCast's example, they could have sold out for $450 million, but later had to settle for $7 million. With Strategic Entrepreneurism the goal is to sell your company for a large amount as soon as possible. It is not to shoot for that once in a lifetime opportunity of trying to become the next Google or Microsoft, where your odds of success drop dramatically with each year. PointCast found this out the hard way.

The Trap of First-Mover Advantage

Being the first product in the market is a nice advantage, but rarely a crucial one. The world is littered with failed companies that had first-mover advantage but lost it because of their own mistakes or through superior competition. Having first-mover advantage is no benefit at all if that's the only advantage your company has over others.

Allen Weiss, a marketing professor at USC's Marshall School of Business, points out that historically first movers have failed in a number of industries. "Have you ever heard of Fitch's shampoo, Chux disposable diapers, Reychler laundry detergent, or Bright Star batteries?" asks Weiss. "These were all market trailblazers at one time, and they're all gone."

Weiss cites research showing that 47 percent of all market pioneers fail. "Only a few of the ones that don't fail—11 percent is the estimate—maintain a market leader position several years later," he says.

The first spreadsheet in the world was a product called VisiCalc, created by a company called VisiCorp. After gathering a massive following with its first-mover advantage, VisiCalc soon got wiped out when a newer and far superior spreadsheet program came out called Lotus 1-2-3. For years, Lotus 1-2-3 dominated the spreadsheet market until Microsoft Excel came along and knocked Lotus 1-2-3 out of its dominant position.

These days hardly anyone has heard of, let alone uses, either VisiCalc or Lotus 1-2-3. The problem is that first-mover advantage can give you a head start, but it can't help you maintain that head start. By relying too much on a first-mover advantage for your company's success, you risk overlooking the importance of creating a quality product that can sustain your company over the long-term.

The Trap of Missing the Holy Grail of Problems

Netflix originally sold DVDs by mail. This business model made money, but it didn't address the Holy Grail problem of watching movies. The real problem surrounding movies wasn't having a hard time buying DVDs. The real Holy Grail problem was having a limited selection of DVDs to choose when you wanted to rent a movie.

Since traditional brick and mortar video stores have limited storage space they tend to stock only the most profitable DVD rentals. Such a focus on stocking high-profit merchandise means it's always easy to rent the latest movies, but much harder to rent older, more obscure movies.

Netflix solved this problem by offering a video store that not only offers an unlimited selection of all possible movies, but allows subscribers to hold on to a movie as long as they wish without the risk of late fees. By solving the Holy Grail problem of renting movies, Netflix has grown to a dominant position in the market place.

Compare the fortunes of Netflix with Hollywood Video, a traditional brick and mortar video rental store that was once the largest competitor to Blockbuster Video. Like Blockbuster Video, Hollywood Video operated physical retail space, which meant they tended to stock an abundance of the latest movies at the sacrifice of storing older movies. If customers wanted to rent an older movie, their chances of finding it at Hollywood Video were no different from finding it at Blockbuster Video.

Essentially Hollywood Video did nothing more than duplicate Blockbuster Video, right down to the limited rental selection and late fees. In other words, Hollywood Video ignored the Holy Grail problem of renting movies while Netflix tackled that Holy Grail problem head-on. The results are obvious. Netflix is thriving while Hollywood Video is shutting down stores.

Too many entrepreneurs start a company that solves a problem, but it's not a Holy Grail type of problem. Identifying and solving a Holy Grail problem is crucial for your company's success and long-term survival. Failing to solve a Holy Grail problem puts your entire company at risk. If your company isn't solving a Holy Grail type of problem, your company most likely won't be around long.

GROWTH PHASE FAILURES

Initially every startup begins in debt, either owing money to the founders, who may have put up their own money, or owing money to outside investors. Once a company survives the initial startup phase, it enters the growth phase where the company slowly builds customers and struggles to earn a profit.

The Trap of Missing a Strategic Customer

As a general rule, it's more profitable to sell to other businesses than it is to sell to individuals. While companies like Amazon.com have built an entire business around catering to individuals, selling to one business will generate more revenue than selling to one person.

Amp'd Mobile, a mobile phone service started in 2005, discovered the problem of targeting individuals rather than businesses. Since the company focused solely on expanding a large customer base as fast as possible, Amp'd Mobile made it easy for customers to subscribe to their service. Where rival mobile phone services accepted only customers who could be expected to pay their bills in 30 days or less, Amp'd Mobile relaxed these restrictions. It eagerly allowed customers to take up to 90 days to pay their bills, accepting a much higher percentage of risky customers who had been turned down by other mobile phone services.

The end result was predictable. After spending over $360 million in funding, the company declared bankruptcy. The problem wasn't that the company didn't offer a desirable service, but that up to 80,000 of the company's 175,000 customers were unable to pay their bills. By deluding themselves that a growing customer base was the most important goal, Amp'd Mobile forgot the basic rule in business: If your customers don't pay their bills, it doesn't matter how many customers you have.

Even if your customers can pay their bills, selling to a single person generally won't help you sell to a second person, but selling to a single business can often help you sell to a second business. Many companies make the mistake of diluting their resources to chase after any customer. What companies should do, especially when they're growing, is to focus their resources on a customer who can help increase the chances of making future sales easier.

Every industry has its own strategic customers, but an attractive strategic customer should include:

- ○ A reputation that can validate your product

- ○ A business relationship with other potential customers

- ○ A potentially large source of revenue from this single customer

One factor to consider is that a strategic customer isn't necessarily the largest or most profitable customer, but this is the trap that many entrepreneurs make. When your company needs to generate revenue, most entrepreneurs are seduced into chasing after the biggest customer with the largest amount of revenue. What's more important is chasing after the customer who can make it easier for you to make additional sales.

If you had a computer product and your first customer was Microsoft or IBM, it would be easy to make additional sales based on the validation that Microsoft or IBM gives to your product. Ironically, a large company can also be a small customer. If a company like Microsoft or IBM only needs to purchase a small number of your products, you could end up making less money than if you had pursued a smaller company with a greater need for your products.

However, selling to a smaller company often won't validate your product in the eyes of the market. Gain Starbucks or Google as a customer and you'll immediately attract the interest of similar potential customers. Gain a smaller customer that most people have never heard of and you may make more money from it initially, but it won't help you to expand your market.

Besides having a good reputation, a strategic customer should ideally have connections to other potential customers. You could sell the same product to two different banks, but one bank may have already established business relationships with a mortgage broker, a mutual fund manager, and an accounting firm. These all could be potential customers for your product.

Gaining this bank as a customer would be a strategic decision, since you would now have an easier time selling your product to all of these potential customers. Because selling is all about relationships, don't look to sell to individual customers. Look to sell to a single company that's part of an established network, and make that company your strategic customer.

The Trap of Running Out of Money

Avoid the trap of having your company need as much money as possible before it can turn a profit. While every company needs money to get started, keep your debt as low as possible. Remember, every time you accept additional funding your company needs to earn back that same amount before it can turn a profit. Eventually there comes a point where accepting additional funding simply sinks your company deeper into a debt from which it can never recover.

In the end, the main purpose of any company is to provide a product to sell to others; anything else is ultimately irrelevant. Unfortunately, many entrepreneurs forget this basic business rule. Instead of spending their seed capital on equipment or people who can create the product, they'll waste that money leasing fancy office spaces, buying expensive office furniture, or providing perks for the executives. As a general rule, if you're spending money on anything that won't directly help your company produce a product that it can sell, you're probably wasting money. When you run out of money your company has failed. The fastest way too many companies fail is by spending their capital on luxuries instead of spending it on creating and marketing a product.

Another way that companies can quickly fail is when their sales don't equal or surpass their expenses. If your company can't generate a profit, it doesn't matter how wonderful your product may be; eventually you will go broke.

DeNovis Software once created a program for handling medical claims. After raising over $125 million in venture capital, they took longer than expected to develop and test their software. With no revenue coming in until the product could be completed, the company simply ran out of money before they could finish their program, forcing the company to declare bankruptcy.

The Trap of Growing Too Fast

Every startup wants to grow, but there's a huge difference between manageable growth and runaway growth. Manageable growth allows a company to adapt to servicing additional customers, whether this requires hiring more technical support or sales staff, or increasing production.

The alternative to manageable growth is rampant growth, where the company expands so rapidly that its infrastructure can't support this growth. The result is that the company eventually collapses from its own weight.

For example, sales may be skyrocketing, but fulfilling those orders may get backlogged, upsetting impatient customers. If the company tries to rush additional products, quality control might suffer, resulting in angry customers and a sagging reputation in the market. The longer the company allows its sullied reputation to linger, the fewer customers it will have and the greater the opportunities will be for its competitors.

Eventually the company has to trim expenses by reducing sales staff or technical personnel, further accelerating the downward decline of the company and its inability to attract new customers. Yet all of these problems could have been avoided by focusing not just on growth, but on obtaining strategic customers.

In 1999 AllAdvantage tried to tap into the growing online advertising market by offering an Internet service that paid users 50 cents an hour to watch banner ads. The company grew rapidly as subscribers eagerly signed up to get paid to surf the Internet. Unfortunately the company's revenues from advertising never kept pace with the growing customer base that the company needed to keep paying to view online advertisements. Once online advertising revenue dried up, AllAdvantage failed, and took over $135 million in venture capital down the drain.

Theoretically, you want as many customers as possible to generate revenue. Since realistically, you will never have the resources you need to satisfy all possible customers, you really need to focus on picking the customers you want and need. When your company takes the initiative to choose its customers, you can manage your company's growth while choosing only those customers that can help you in both the short-term and the long-term.

SCALING PHASE FAILURES

The scaling phase occurs when a company has developed a customer base and begins to expand. Ideally, this is the time when your company has established itself as a leader in its field. This is also the time when you have a choice: Continue to grow or look into being acquired.

Ideally, the startup phase should take one year, the growth phase should take another year, and the scaling phase should take a third year. This is the time when entrepreneurs often take a thriving company and risk driving it into the ground by making the following types of mistakes:

The Trap of the Wrong Type of Funding

Every startup can spend more money, but that doesn't mean that every startup will spend that money wisely. When accepting money from investors, accept money only from certain types of investors. Accept money from the wrong type of investors and you risk losing your company.

Here's the problem. Outside investors often look for a quick, massive return on their investment. As a result, if they don't see a company returning a profit fast enough, they'll often push for control of that company by adding their own people to the board of directors. This allows the investor to control the company and make decisions which may be profitable in the short-term, but fatal to the company's survival in the long-term. Since the investors have only a short-term focus, they simply want a quick payoff in the shortest amount of time.

Sometimes outside investors will even resort to firing the company's founders, essentially taking the company away from the entrepreneur. At this point all your hard work as an entrepreneur can be lost, since the outside investor often pushes the company to grow too fast in an effort to churn a quick profit. Too many times this push for massive short-term profits backfires and the company fails, taking the investor's money down with it.

When accepting any outside money from investors, the amount of money should always be your last consideration. First, you want an investor who can help your company thrive. Often a potential customer will invest in a company to insure that a product is built to solve their most pressing needs (the Holy Grail problem).

Besides looking for funding from potential customers, look for investors who can provide critical business connections to other companies. For example, many angel investors are former entrepreneurs themselves. And many venture capitalists specialize in funding companies in certain sectors such as the telecommunications sector or the alternative energy sector. As a result, both types of investors will likely have contacts with other companies who could be potential customers or business partners.

Such investors can then provide an easier path to new customers or investors, allowing your company to receive funding and tap into an existing network of business relationships that can help the company grow.

More importantly, outside investors with experience in your company's field are likely to be more understanding of the problems your company faces, and less likely to demand a quick return on their investment. Such investors will be more likely to nurture your company to profitability and sustainable growth.

Given the choice between accepting money from someone who demands a quick return on his or her investment, or someone willing to help your company thrive and willing to be more patient in getting a return, which type of investor would you rather be indebted to?

The Trap of the IPO

The dream of many entrepreneurs is to take a company public through an initial public offering (IPO) and raise millions of dollars in the process. The trap is thinking that an IPO alone is the goal of a company. In truth, an IPO is just another form of outside funding. Just because a company achieves a successful IPO doesn't mean that the company can't fail later.

An IPO defines a value for a company, but it's only useful if the company's stock price increases. Many companies have been offered an IPO, only to watch the price of their stock plummet immediately afterwards. Now the entrepreneur may own thousands of shares of the company's stock, but that stock may be nearly worthless if the stock price plummets too far.

The problem is in looking at an IPO as an end result. Just reaching the point of an IPO offering is noteworthy since so few companies achieve it. But the company must still perform and grow after its IPO. Focusing solely on an IPO can lead companies to push a company too fast toward an IPO while neglecting its core business.

An IPO is not the end result. It is just another stepping stone towards greater profitability. As an entrepreneur, your goal shouldn't be taking your company public, but making your company as profitable as possible—whether that involves going public through an IPO, staying private, or being acquired by another company. An IPO is one way to return value to your investors, but it's not the only way. The sooner you focus on making money anyway you can, the less likely you'll see an IPO as the magic wand that can solve your financial problems overnight.

The Trap of the Problem of Growth in a Changing Market

Luck can play a role in the success of any company, but luck can work against a company too. One reason why selling your company to another company is so attractive is that it guarantees a return on your investment. Trying to grow and maintain a company means dealing with the ongoing risk that your company may still go out of business anyway because of changing market conditions.

Back in the '90s, Iomega made a fortune selling a portable storage solution called Zip drives. To use a Zip drive, you needed to buy Zip disks. At the time, consumers and businesses eagerly snapped up Zip drives for backing up their files. During this time, Iomega's stock soared.

Then the market changed. What made Zip drives and Zip disks so popular was that hard disks remained relatively expensive. However, once the cost of hard disks began to plummet, the cost of a buying a second hard drive was equal to or even less than the cost of buying a Zip drive and Zip disks. Plus, buying a second hard drive meant more storage space than a Zip disk could offer.

The rapid drop in price for hard disks meant that the market for Zip drives and Zip disks dried up overnight. Iomega's stock plummeted and the company spent the next few years limping along until they were finally acquired by EMC Corporation for a far lower price than it was worth at its peak.

The lesson is that the longer you hold on to your company, the more risk you incur. Hold on to a company too long and its value could plummet dramatically, which means all your hard work in starting and running a company all those years could be far less than you wish. If you had designed your company to be acquired, you could have cashed out much earlier, received a high value for your company, and had free time to pursue other interests.

You don't want to be left stuck running a dying company in a suddenly hostile market where your company has little hope of ever attaining its once lofty status as a profitable company.

The Trap of Being the Founder

Perhaps the most tragic result is when a company fails through self-inflicted wounds. This often occurs because entrepreneurs are often more talented at starting up a company than they are at managing a company. As a result, an entrepreneur risks staying too long in a company and making decisions that can literally kill that company.

At one time, Gateway Computers was a major mail-order manufacturer of personal computers. After growing from a small mail-order company, the company went through a successful IPO where its stock peaked at a high of $84 a share in late 1999. Unfortunately, the company founders, who proved so adept at starting up a mail-order computer business, made several critical mistakes in trying to grow their business.

First, they opened a chain of retail stores, which increased costs without increasing revenue. Second, they branched out into consumer electronics. Instead of focusing on selling Gateway computers, the company tried to sell Gateway television sets and

	Old Rules	New Rules
Startup Phase	❏ Focus on the product.	❏ Focus on the problem.
	❏ Focus on being first to the market.	❏ Focus on identifying the correct market.
	❏ Focus on solving any problem.	❏ Focus on solving a Holy Grail problem.
Growth Phase	❏ Sell to any customers	❏ Only sell to strategic customers.
	❏ Use outside funding to grow the company to profitabilitiy.	❏ Collaborate with customers to grow the company to profitability.
	❏ Grow as fast as possible.	❏ Only grow as fast as your increased profits allow.
Scaling Phase	❏ Accept any outside funding.	❏ Only accept outside funding from investors willing to be patient for a return on their investment and who can provide guidance or connections to help your company sell more products.
	❏ Design the company towards an IPO.	❏ Design a company to be acquired.
	❏ Create a product and find a way to sell it.	❏ Find a market and create a product that the market will buy.
Long-Term Goal	❏ Hold on to a company until it becomes a massive success.	❏ Stay in a company until you can sell it at a profit.

Table 8-1. Comparison of Old and New Rules of Running a Company

other high-end electronics. This also sapped the company's resources without giving them a corresponding boost in revenue.

The struggling company soon closed all its retail stores, aban-
doned its entry into the consumer electronics market, and
returned to its personal computer mail-order roots—only to

find it had been far surpassed by its competitors. In 2007 the company agreed to be acquired by Acer Corporation, which paid the equivalent of $1.90 a share for the entire company, a far cry from its once lofty stock price of $84 a share.

The nature of any business is that the longer you run a company, the more likely you'll make a critical mistake that could drive your company into the ground. The goal of starting up any company is to make money. The longer you hold on to your company, the more you risk that your company will drop in value. The sooner you can sell your company, the more likely you'll earn a hefty profit for your efforts in the shortest amount of time. That's what Strategic Entrepreneurism is really all about.

9

Calculating Success

A successful startup is a function of time as well as the total money returned to investors and employees. Most people judge a startup only by the money it returns to its investors. This is why so many companies continue to receive funding even as their prospects for success grow dimmer every day. After sinking millions into a startup, investors often hope that they'll get their money back, and perhaps a small return, if only they wait long enough.

What usually happens is that the longer they wait, the lower the company's valuation drops until the company is eventually worth a fraction of what was expected. In the meantime, the investors have not only lost their money, but also have lost time focusing on a doomed startup.

That's why you must consider both time and money when measuring success. Basically you want to make as much money as possible in the shortest amount of time possible. Generally there are several possible outcomes based on time and money:

○ Making a lot of money over a long period of time. (This is what defines major successes such as Google, Amazon.com, and eBay. This kind of success often takes ten years.)

○ Making a moderate amount of money over a short period of time. (This is the goal of Strategic Entrepreneurism when you sell your company to an acquirer. The typical time frame for this is between three to five years.)

○ Making a moderate amount of money over a long period of time. (This occurs when a company achieves profitability and can be considered a minor success. However, such moderately successful companies can rarely achieve major profitability in the future, but do risk losing their profitability from changing market conditions. This type of company is equivalent to treading water. (You may not be drowning, but you aren't achieving any massive success either.)

○ Losing money over a long period of time. (This occurs when companies show promise, but cannot achieve profitability. What happens is that investors continue to sink money into the company to keep it afloat long enough for it to eventually fail.)

○ Losing a lot of money in a short period of time. (This is the classic startup failure that arrives with hype and massive funding and then disappears in a few years because of a faulty, unsustainable business model.)

As an entrepreneur your goal is to maximize your company's value so that you and your investors make money. Initially an entrepreneur begins with an idea. To turn this idea into reality, the entrepreneur needs the help of others. Each person the entrepreneur adds to his or her team obtains a percentage of the company, which is why it's important to keep your team to a minimum and only add people who can contribute value to your startup. The more people you add to your team, the lower the percentage of the company remains for everyone, so it's in everyone's best interests to keep a team as lean as possible.

Initially the two most important people in any startup are the entrepreneur and the person capable of making or developing your product (who may not always be the entrepreneur). The other people on your team may be necessary for attracting additional funding, lending credibility to your company, providing your startup with the necessary business contacts, or providing marketing experience and sales skills.

CALCULATING OWNERSHIP

In the beginning, the startup's founders own 100 percent of the company. If the founders can raise their own funding and grow the company from its initial profits, the founders can retain complete control over the company. Most likely, the founders will need seed capital to help them get started.

Outside funding usually works by either charging you interest (and expecting you to pay the debt off within a fixed period of time), or by taking a financial stake in your company. Banks typically loan money to companies while venture capital firms take an equity stake in your company.

The key is to accept only the funding that you need to retain as much control over your company as possible. A simple formula for calculating the percentage of ownership the founders retain is as follows:

$$F = F_0 * (1 - L)$$
Where F = Founders' latest % ownership
F_0 = Founders' previous % ownership
L = Outside investor's % ownership

In a new startup, the value of $F_0 = 1.0$ and $L = 0$, so the formula is as follows:

$$F = 1.0 * (1 - 0)$$
$$= 1.0 * 1$$
$$= 1.0 \text{ (or 100\%)}$$

In exchange for providing seed capital, outside investors want a percentage of the company. Suppose that outside investors provide seed capital in exchange for 25% (0.25) of the company. The remainder of the company's ownership is now calculated as follows:

$$F = 1.0 * (1 - 0.25)$$
$$= 1.0 * 0.75$$
$$= 0.75 \text{ (or 75\%)}$$

When outside investors take 25% ownership of the company, the remaining 75% is left in the hands of the founders. Now each round of additional funding requires exchanging capital for a percentage of the company. So if a company goes through a second round of funding where these additional investors accept a 10% stake in the company, the formula calculates the diluted ownership for the founders using these values:

F = Founders' latest % ownership
F_0 = 0.75 (Founders' previous % ownership)
L = 0.10 (Outside investor's % ownership)

Inserting these new values into the formula calculates the following result:

$$F = 0.75 * (1 - 0.10)$$
$$= 0.75 * 0.90$$
$$= 0.675 \text{ (or 67.5\%)}$$

With each additional round of funding, the ownership percentage of the founders gets less and less, which is called dilution. The more funding your company requires, the less ownership of the company is left for you.

If a company goes through too many rounds of financing, their percentage of company ownership can sink below the ownership percentage of any outside investors. When this happens, it's possible for the outside investors to take over the company, fire the founding team, and put their own people in charge of the company instead. This creates zero value for the founders and rewards them with a trivial payoff for all their hard work.

To retain control over your company, you have several options:

- ○ Start up your company as inexpensively as possible, relying on high-technology to leverage your company's reach and strength

- ○ Only accept as much outside funding as necessary

- ○ Grow organically; let your company's profits fund your growth

Exchanging partial ownership of your company for funding is inevitable. How much funding you accept and how much ownership you're willing to give away is negotiable, so choose wisely.

CALCULATING SUCCESS

As we have seen, a company's success is a function of time and money. The more money involved, the less important the time. After all, you might be willing to wait three years to earn $1 million dollars, but you might be willing to wait ten years if you knew you could earn $40 million dollars.

Eventually time plays an important role because getting $1 billion dollars is worthless if you have to wait an inordinate amount of time (such as 1,000 years) in order to get it. The key to defining success isn't solely in the amount of money but by an optimum balance of time and money. Just as $1 billion dollars is useless if you have to wait 1,000 years to get it, so will a short period of time be worthless if it only returns a trivial amount of money. There are many ways to think about the optimum balance between time and money.

In the stock market, traders use a mathematical formula, called the Black-Scholes model, which calculates the price of a stock option taking into account time, risk and volatility. This complex Black-Scholes formula estimates what a stock option should be worth at a fixed moment of time in the future, based on the current stock price and its current growth rate.

In the world of startups, you can apply the same thought process to estimate the value of a company as a function of time. Rather than focus solely on value (a fixed dollar amount), you must also focus on the time needed to acquire that fixed dollar amount.

Suppose an engineer works for a company that grants stock options worth $1 million dollars after four years. If another company offers to acquire that company after 18 months, offering the engineer $400,000, should the engineer wait four years for the $1 million dollar payout or accept the $400,000 payout at only 18 months?

Simple math can provide the answer. Dividing $1 million dollars by four years equates to 48 monthly payments of $20,833. Within an 18 month period, a monthly payment of $20,833 multiplied by 18 returns $375,000, which is much less than the guaranteed $400,000 offered to the engineer if the company is sold after 18 months. In other words, the shorter time period of 18 months is actually more profitable than the longer time period that returns $1 million dollars.

The function of time places a big uncertainty on the value of any company. If a company offers to acquire your company after 18 months, the price paid may be greater than the value of the company over time. However, the value of a company over time is an unknown variable.

If in four years your company increases in value, the engineer might receive $2 million dollars rather than $1 million dollars. However, if the company drops in value after four years the engineer might receive less than $1 million dollars, or even nothing at all.

An early acquisition of your company at the right price can return a greater payoff on a monthly basis than waiting much longer for that amount of profit. Selling your company gives you a guaranteed return on your investment. At the right price, this payoff will often be much greater than your company's estimated value in the long-term.

The risk is selling your company too soon or at too low a price. You can always negotiate on price, but you won't necessarily know what your company could be worth several years from now.

In general, the longer you hold on to a company, the greater the risks you'll encounter from changing market conditions. Nobody wants to sell a company too soon when it could blossom into the next Google or eBay. However appealing this idea may be, the fact that nine out of ten startups fail, make the odds of turning your company into tomorrow's next big success story remote. The choice essentially boils down to two options:

○ Hold on to your company and attempt to turn it into a big success

○ Sell your company early and take the guaranteed payout

If nine out of ten startups fail, out of that ten percent that succeed, an even smaller number turn out to be tremendously successful. The majority of startups survive in various degrees of monetary success, but the longer you hold on to a company, the function of time increases, lowering the ultimate value of your company on a monthly basis.

Strategic Entrepreneurism supports the idea that selling your company within a short time period returns a greater value as a function of both money and time.

THE BASICS OF STRATEGIC ENTREPRENEURISM

A Harvard Business School study found that 93 percent of all companies emerged (at exit) with a completely different strategy from what they had initially set out to implement. Furthermore, the study found that it took four to five years for a company to discover the right product and business model.

A Crescent Ventures study concluded that "a funding strategy that deploys capital incrementally while the business model is sharpened and the market is better understood" is infinitely preferable to a strategy that releases the funds in more conventional large amounts. The common thread is iteration. Receiving additional capital should be dependent on achieving specific company milestones. Good teams iterate products as quickly as they can learn from their customers. Good businesses change their strategies.

What this means is that the average startup releases a product, and then modifies its product and business model gradually over the next five years until it discovers the optimum business strategy. This approach is inefficient and more like blindly groping in the dark until you stumble across the optimum business model.

Strategic Entrepreneurism essentially reverse engineers each step. Instead of starting with a product and business model and gradually shaping it through multiple iterations, Strategic Entrepreneurism begins with the specific goal of having your company acquired by another company. To achieve this you should:

○ Decide the type of business and product a larger company would most likely want to acquire.

	Old Rules	New Rules
Time	❏ Grow a company as fast as possible	❏ Grow a company as fast as its profits can keep up with its growth.
	❏ Hold on to a company until it either succeeds or fails	❏ Sell a company within 3 to 5 years.
Money	❏ Accept as much funding as possible to speed up growth.	❏ Accept as little funding as possible to avoid dilution of ownership.
	❏ Try to turn the company into a dominant, billion dollar leader.	❏ Try to turn the company into an attractive acquisition target.
Long-Term Result	❏ 9 out of 10 companies fail, but the one success earns enough profit to make up for the other nine failures.	❏ At least 5 out of 10 companies earn a modest profit and one or more may be sold for a large amount.

Table 9-1. Comparison of Old and New Rules of Looking at Time and Money

○ Create that product in collaboration with a strategic customer that a potential acquirer finds attractive.

○ Put together a team of people that provide skills necessary to create your product or run your company while also providing contacts to a potential acquirer.

○ Start up your company with as little outside funding as possible using high-technology to keep costs to a minimum.

Under Strategic Entrepreneurism, you aren't guessing what the market might want and wasting time for five years continually modifying your product for acceptance. Instead, you're collaborating with the customer to create the exact product needed right away.

The goal is to sell your company. By beginning with this goal, you work backwards so that everything you do brings you one step closer to achieving that goal. By steering straight toward your goal, you're more likely to reach it than a similar startup that fumbles around, constantly redefining its product and business model until it stumbles across one that works.

Success, as defined by Strategic Entrepreneurism, involves choosing a goal and reaching it within a period of three to five years to maximize your company's return on its investment. Strategic Entrepreneurism does nothing more than to give you the maximum chance for success with a minimal waste of time or money.

10

Thoughts

On April 18, 1922 John Johnson invented the adjustable wrench. What's amazing is that it took over 70 years after the industrial revolution for someone to think up the seemingly obvious idea of an adjustable wrench. Until this invention people were forced to own different size wrenches, yet one simple invention solved that problem overnight.

More than 70 years after the adjustable wrench, I had this same sense of amazement when I first realized my own idea for my company. The main difference between my idea and the adjustable wrench was that my tool existed only online

The problem was that the Internet focused too much on communication and not enough on security. To tackle this Holy Grail problem of online security authentication, I focused on how to make online security available instantly and inexpensively to millions of users—no matter which type of computer they may be using.

The company I co-founded to solve this problem was called Bharosa, which means "trust" in the Hindi language. To form Bharosa, I recruited the best people I could find to fulfill specific functions, which made me feel a lot like the character of Dapper Danny Ocean (George Clooney) in the movie "Ocean's Eleven."

In the movie Danny Ocean has been released for less than 24 hours on parole from a New Jersey penitentiary and he's already plotting his next plan. By following his three rules—don't hurt anybody, don't steal from anyone who doesn't deserve it, and play the game like you've got nothing to lose—Danny orchestrates the most sophisticated, elaborate casino heist in history.

To help him pull this heist, Danny recruits a handpicked 11-man crew of specialists including an ace card sharp (Brad Pitt), a master pickpocket (Matt Damon) and a demolition genius (Don Cheadle), who will attempt to steal over $150 million from three Las Vegas casinos owned by Terry Benedict (Andy Garcia), the elegant, ruthless entrepreneur who just happens to be dating Danny's ex-wife Tess (Julia Roberts).

Although creating a startup isn't quite as dramatic as planning a multimillion dollar heist on a heavily guarded casino, the idea is still the same. Find the most talented people you need and put them together on the same team. Then find some mentors who have knowledge and experience identical or similar to yours, perhaps with success in their own startups, and let them point you in the right direction while telling you what to avoid. This is the way we started Bharosa.

The tool that Bharosa created consisted of an Authenticator and a Tracker. The Authenticator product provided various personalized pinpads and keyboards that appeared onscreen for greater password security. By clicking on the onscreen keyboard, you can type in a password without using keystrokes, which could be captured by a keystroke logger.

Besides preventing a hacker from watching a person type in keystrokes, the Authenticator product also verifies when you're logged on to the correct website when you enter your password. The program also includes tools that protect the way your data gets stored on the browser before it's encrypted by standard Internet security.

The Tracker product essentially replaced smart cards and one time password generating tokens that users normally had to carry around (and risk losing). Tracker identifies users by their computer, using the computer's unique Internet Protocol (IP) address and a variety of other attributes enabling a software-only approach to strong security. This software was a key player in what became known as the fraud detection sector.

Once we knew the type of Holy Grail problem to solve and the people needed to create and market this product, the final two steps involved designing the company to be acquired and finding a strategic customer.

Initially, I decided that the type of company most likely to acquire Bharosa would be a computer company that either specialized in security or needed it as part of its own services. That limited the potential list of acquirers to a handful of the major computer security players including RSA, VeriSign, IBM, Symantec, McAfee, Computer Associates, and Oracle. Other potential, but lesser known acquirers included Fair Isaac, SAS Institute, and ActivIdentity.

After I had a list of potential acquirers, the next step was to focus on those customers who would be most strategic to this short list of potential acquirers. In other words,

Just to give you an idea of how heated the competition was for online security products at the time I formed Bharosa, here's a list of all of Bharosa's competitors. By the time you read this, some of these companies will likely have gone out of business while others might have merged with another company.

3i Infotech
41st Parameter
Actimize
CardCops
Corillian
Covelight
Cydelity
Debix
Digital Resolve
ECtel
Edentify
EMC/RSA
Entrust
Fair Isaac
First Data Corp.
Forent,
ID Analytics
i-flex solutions
iovation
LifeLock
MarkMonitor
Norkom Technologies
Pentaho (Weka)
Retail Decisions
SAS Institute
StrikeForce Technologies

ThreatMatrix
TrustedID
and
VeriSign

The reason Bharosa became a success was nothing more than applying the rules of Strategic Entrepreneurism. As the 451 Group (www.451group.com), a website dedicated to covering business enterprise IT innovation, said in analyzing the crowded online security market:

"A couple of pure-play vendors stand out to us at this point. Bharosa, which says it's taken about $2m in external funding, has products for multifactor authentication and device biometrics, risk analysis and anti-fraud and has just announced a fraud net it says is being tested with several beta customers. Through third-party reporting, announced customer wins, Bharosa's statements about customers and revenue, and off-the-record comments from its competitors, we'd say Bharosa is the pure-play horse to beat. "

I needed a list of companies that would be ideal customers for a company like IBM, Oracle, or Symantec, not necessarily an ideal customer for Bharosa.

This meant exercising discipline in focusing Bharosa's limited resources into pursuing those strategic customers at the expense of ignoring non-strategic customers, who still represented critical revenue opportunities. While the short term opportunities might have favored non-strategic customers, the long-term benefits favored strategic customers.

In designing Bharosa's products, Authenticator and Tracker, we made sure that the technology could be infinitely scalable so that it could be integrated easily within a much larger company (a potential acquirer). While it might have been more cost-effective in the short-term to design a product without allowing it to be scalable in the future, this would have severely limited Bharosa's appeal to a potential acquirer. Thus Bharosa sank much of its limited resources in building scalable technology for the future.

Since our product was software-based, its physical costs were negligible; the majority of our expenses stemmed from the cost of equipment and labor. Such limited expenses allowed us to start the company with minimal outside funding, allowing the founding team to retain well over 50 percent ownership. This allowed us to control the company and make decisions without needing to gain the approval of others.

What made Bharosa attractive to a potential acquirer wasn't just its technology, but the high percentage of talented engineering personnel that were part of the company. Any potential acquirer would get a superior product backed up by an excellent engineering design team.

Finally, before we even considered selling to a potential acquirer, we made sure that Bharosa generated a profit. When your company offers a superior product, you'll probably catch the attention of a potential acquirer, but if your company offers a superior product and already earns a profit selling that product, you'll definitely catch the attention of a potential acquirer.

Instead of a potential acquirer looking at your company as a quick way to gain the rights to a product, they'll look at your company as an instant source of guaranteed revenue.

Finding Bharosa's strategic customer was more a matter of knowing the market from a personal point of view. Wells Fargo had been my bank since I went to college and I knew everything about their online applications. The Wells Fargo Internet Services executives were based in San Francisco, so they were easily approachable since I lived in the Bay area as well.

I also knew that Wells Fargo is considered an early adopter of technology that loves startups. I could feel this walking into the first Wells Fargo presentation. There were cubicles and office toys and a startup feeling among the entire corporation.

In comparison, a company such as the mutual fund manager Vanguard, had a completely different feel. They had sailboats and oil paintings in the lobby along with brochures on the coffee table, confirming that the company has grown to be one of the

The basic business model of Bharosa was focused on risk-based authorization, which is an approach developed mainly in the financial industry. The idea is to observe and analyze user interactions to detect potential attacks and other dangerous situations. If there is a risk, the authorization to access a specific system or specific data within in a system is denied.

The field of online security was crowded with at least 30 different companies offering some form of a security product that competed directly with Bharosa, ranging from fraud detection (FD), anti-money laundering (AML) detection, device biometrics (DB), or identity theft prevention (ITP).

Fraud detection identifies phishing scams designed to trick users into giving their passwords. Anti-money laundering compares transactions to spot relationships between individuals or entities, and "behaviors of interest" transactions carried out by suspicious parties or by people in geographically high-risk regions. Device biometrics relies on devices to verify a

largest mutual funds in the country without acquiring a single company. That's when I knew the battle was over before it began. When I starting presenting our solution, some guy on the phone interrupted after 90 seconds to ask how many employees we had.

Just by visiting potential strategic customers, I could get a feel for whether the corporate culture would be open to collaborating with Bharosa.

After I identified a strategic customer for Bharosa (Wells Fargo) and a list of potential acquirers (IBM, VeriSign, SAS Institute, etc.), I made sure that everything Bharosa did, from its technology, its founding team, and its customers, would integrate smoothly into any larger company. A potential acquirer could examine Bharosa and find that everything was primed to be bought out and return profits right away. Basically, I wanted to make Bharosa so attractive that a larger company could literally not afford not to buy out the company. Rather than compete against Bharosa, larger companies would do a cost-analysis and find that it was less expensive and more profitable just to acquire the company instead. When I reached this point with the company, I knew that Bharosa's success was assured.

Two days that I'll always remember for the rest of my life are the day we launched the Bharosa solution for Wells Fargo and the day Oracle announced the acquisition of our company. Both days started at 4:30 a.m. and by 9:00 a.m., I had received more unsolicited email than any previous day of my life. Over 100+ Wells Fargo engineers, who had collaborated on our project, offered their congratulations and I received emails from around the world when Oracle announced their acquisition of Bharosa. More than twenty five million people worldwide used Bharosa products at the time of the acquisition.

I made 51 outgoing telephone calls the day of the Oracle deal, primarily to customers and partners, and I received 42 calls. All 93 calls took an average of five minutes apiece, which meant that on that day alone, I spent approximately eight hours of time on the phone. In between phone calls, I sat in a war room and briefed analysts, press and members of

user's authorization, such as a fingerprint or token. Identity theft prevention scours the Internet for stolen information and managed fraud alerts at credit reporting agencies.

One common solution to online security is called single-factor authentication. In one example, customers select an image as "their own" during an initial sign-on process. On subsequent logins, the website displays an array of images including the one initially chosen by the customer. This proves to the customer that the website can be trusted (it displayed the customer's secret image) and proves to the bank that the customer is who he says he is (he selected the correct image).

One problem with this solution is that it's susceptible to man-in-the-middle attacks. By redirecting the customer's Web browser to a malicious website, a skilled attacker can simply act as a proxy between the bank and customer, giving both sides of the transaction the "proof" they need to assume that bidirectional authentication has been accomplished.

Another common solution is to use the customer's computer as an identification token, by embedding the code on the customer's computer. The presence of the code proves it's the customer's machine. Another method passively determines a "fingerprint" of the customer's machine, based on the equipment used in that machine.

Further authentication involves geolocation techniques. If a user knows the password and user name and even the image, but an IP address appears to be accessing this account from a strange location, such as from Moldova, the program flags this transaction as suspicious. Monitoring behavior and correlating it with a user's previous behavior can be yet another authentication process.

Bharosa's solution simply relied on users remembering passwords, as they normally do, but then masking their password using an online interface that could foil hackers who capture keystrokes or even peer over the user's shoulder to see exactly what the user is

the Oracle team. Perhaps the only more hectic and more memorable day of my life was my wedding.

Having my company acquired by Oracle was an experience in itself. Oracle's main headquarters has a trophy case containing a keepsake from each of their acquisitions. We gave them a Bharosa pen and a Bharosa replica of a computer mouse made out of crystal to represent their Bharosa acquisition in their trophy case.

After starting a company from scratch and selling it for millions of dollars three years later, the question I'm most often asked now is, "Why aren't you in Hawaii"? Civilians often ask that question. This is a lot like asking a professional athlete, "Now that you've finally reached the major leagues, why do you keep playing?"

Part of the answer is that I truly enjoy being an entrepreneur. Noted broadcast journalist, Tom Brokaw, summed it up nicely when he said, "It's easy to make a buck but a lot tougher to make difference." That's why I'm still an entrepreneur and still looking for new opportunities. I want to continue making a difference.

When you create a company, you can provide yourself financial security, provide meaningful work for others, and solve pressing problems that the world needs solved. Practicing Strategic Entrepreneurism means returning the most amount of capital to investors and typing. Because hackers were then unable to decipher the keystrokes Bharosa's solution turned out to be a profitable one in a market crowded with other solutions of all kinds. employees in the shortest amount of time while providing a service or product that meets a pressing need. Perhaps one day I will go to Hawaii, but I probably won't stay there because everything I want is where I'm at right now.

I share a beautiful home in Tiburon, California with my entrepreneurial wife, Darla Fisher, who brought her business (Ko'ze, www.getkoze.com) to profitability faster than I ever have been able to with any of my businesses. Perhaps the greatest practitioner of Strategic Entrepreneurism in the family, she has taken no outside investment, even from me.

What's especially important to me is my family life, and that includes being close to my father, a co-author of this book, who studied under Dr. Arthur Schlow at Stanford. Dr. Schlow invented the laser and won the Nobel Prize. Back in the '60s during the height of the Vietnam War, Dr. Schlow wrote a letter to the United States government confirming that my father would be of more service to this country as a physicist than as a soldier. Perhaps I owe my life to one of the world's greatest entrepreneurs and I certainly intend to spend the rest of my life trying to become one.

Once you understand the principles behind Strategic Entrepreneurism, you too can turn your dreams into reality, start up a company, make a lot of money, and more importantly, make a difference as well. I've given you the tools and the guidelines. Now the real power rests with you.

Epilogue

We expect that *Strategic Entrepreneurism* has given you the tools to succeed as an entrepreneur. We have examined how to recruit top talent for your organization. There is still an area that bears further examination in my next book, and that is the crucial role of education in producing top talent.

It used to be that the state of the American education system was something you could often hear lamented in the teachers' lounge, but not very often in the board room.

Who could blame entrepreneurs for placing education low on their hierarchy of concerns? From Gates to Zuckerberg, the list seemed only to be growing longer with names of impressive people who had proven education irrelevant to their successful quest to change the world. That is, until now.

Entrepreneurs have recently started to stand up and take notice of a new era upon us, an era in which the next great commercial successes will be in industries like energy and power. Here the breakthroughs will be highly technical in nature and will be attained only by people with genuinely superior expertise and ingenuity in their fields.

There certainly won't be any shortcuts in this new model. To be sure, the days aren't gone in which a dropout can change the future of business with a line of computer code. But increasingly the success of American industry—and indeed, the fate of the world's future—depends upon training and educating people who have the skills to crack substantially more complex codes of science and engineering, such as how to harness nuclear energy, how to deliver clean energy and how to desalinize water, to name just a few.

In other words, the rules for success in industry are changing to depend far more heavily on our education system, which was once the finest in the world, but is today on the brink of collapse.

My next book will examine what will need to be done to restore our American universities to world leadership, as they participate in the battleground for our industrial preeminence in the 21st century and beyond.

GERALD A. FISHER